Penny Dreadfuls

Penny Dreadfuls

The Circulation Patterns of a Victorian Popular Genre

Manon Burz-Labrande

ANTHEM PRESS

Anthem Press
An imprint of Wimbledon Publishing Company
www.anthempress.com

This edition first published in UK and USA 2026
by ANTHEM PRESS
75–76 Blackfriars Road, London SE1 8HA, UK
or PO Box 9779, London SW19 7ZG, UK
and
244 Madison Ave #116, New York, NY 10016, USA

© 2026 Manon Burz-Labrande

The author asserts the moral right to be identified as the author of this work.

All rights reserved. Without limiting the rights under copyright reserved above, no part of this publication may be reproduced, stored or introduced into a retrieval system, or transmitted, in any form or by any means (electronic, mechanical, photocopying, recording or otherwise), without the prior written permission of both the copyright owner and the above publisher of this book.

British Library Cataloguing-in-Publication Data
A catalogue record for this book is available from the British Library.

Library of Congress Cataloging-in-Publication Data: 2025949116
A catalog record for this book has been requested.

ISBN-13: 978-1-83999-630-6 (Pbk)
ISBN-10: 1-83999-630-7 (Pbk)

Cover credit: The People's Periodical and Family Library vol. 1. no. 1-52 (10 Oct. 1846-2 Oct. 1847), created by Edward Lloyd, p. 115. From the archive of the British Library, shelfmark C.140.c.16.

This title is also available as an eBook.

CONTENTS

List of Figures	vii
Acknowledgements	ix
Introduction: Circulation in and of the Penny Dreadfuls	1
1. From Oral Storytelling to Seriality	13
2. Sensationalism and Entertainment	29
3. The Maze of Metropolitan Life: Urbanising the Gothic	47
4. Consuming the Penny Dreadful in Neo-Victorian Fiction	65
Bibliography	85
Index	95

LIST OF FIGURES

Figure 2.1	Drop-head title of instalment number 7 of *The Sketch-Book by 'Bos'*, i.e. Thomas Peckett Prest, published by Edward Lloyd (p. 49). By permission of the British Library.	31
Figure 2.2	Frontispiece of instalment number 11 of *Nicholas Nickleby*, written by Charles Dickens as 'Boz'. From: Charles Dickens, *The Life and Adventures of Nicholas Nickleby*, inserted between xvi and 1.	32
Figure 2.3	Drop-head title of instalment number 1 of *Nickelas Nickelbery*, written by Thomas Peckett Prest as 'Bos' and published by Edward Lloyd (p. 1). By permission of the British Library.	33
Figure 2.4	Front page illustration of issue 7 of Edward Lloyd's *The People's Periodical and Family Library* (p. 97). By permission of the British Library.	35
Figure 2.5	Front page illustration of issue 8 of Edward Lloyd's *The People's Periodical and Family Library* (p. 113). By permission of the British Library.	36
Figure 2.6	Front page illustration of issue 11 of Edward Lloyd's *The People's Periodical and Family Library* (p. 161). By permission of the British Library.	37
Figure 4.1	Front page of issue n°15,933 of *The Morning Herald*, dated Tuesday, 13 September 1831.	79

ACKNOWLEDGEMENTS

This book is based on a PhD thesis and therefore draws from years of research and exchange. I can only begin by apologising in advance to anyone I might forget to thank here; I am deeply grateful for the many friends and colleagues around the globe who, whether they were ten minutes or ten hours away, have contributed to this process through suggestions, questions, friendly chats or constructive feedback.

I would first like to thank my former PhD supervisor, Sylvia Mieszkowski, for her unfailing support and guidance through the years. Your interest in my ideas, your generosity in sharing your experience, your belief in my skills and your attention to detail have allowed me to grow into a confident researcher. You have never doubted that my work would end up published – and here we are.

Throughout the process, I have been lucky enough to be a part of several research communities that have all been tremendously helpful, too. Fascinating conferences and inspiring researchers have contributed to the development of this book over the years; special thanks go to the Victorian Popular Fiction Association, which has always been particularly welcoming and fosters quality work in an environment where experienced colleagues happily take time for younger researchers. I also would like to express my heartfelt thanks to the academic community of the University of Vienna's Department of English and American Studies for providing such a stimulating and supportive environment for my research, and to the Austrian Academy of Sciences, as the first steps that made the publication of this book possible were funded within the Post-Doc Track Programme of the OeAW.

Finally, I would like to extend my sincere thanks to Kevin A. Morrison for believing in this project, and to the editing team at Anthem Press and reviewers who took the time to read my work and provide precious suggestions, which have greatly helped this manuscript reach its final and improved form.

None of this would have been possible without the love and support of my family, and I cannot quite put into words how grateful I am for their presence. I want to thank my parents, for buying me all the books and for believing in me always, and my brother, whose curiosity, humour and critical mind fostered my own. Finally, the warmest, most loving thanks go to my husband and my son, whom I always want to come home to and whose love has made me the happiest and best version of myself. Mon grand Leo, you already love books, and your wonderful dad has read this one many times in all its different versions – it is not much of a bedtime story, but maybe someday you'll read it too!

Introduction

CIRCULATION IN AND OF THE PENNY DREADFULS

> Ah! thousands on Shockers have fed full,
> And yet *not* of crimes got a head-full.
> Let us put down the vile,
> Yet endeavour the while,
> To be *just* to the poor "Penny Dreadful"!
>
> 'That Poor Penny Dreadful!', *Punch, or the London Charivari* (1895)

The penny dreadfuls' tremendous popularity and active circulation throughout the nineteenth century give rise to fascinating questions: how did the sensational, dreadful stories meet with such success and why were they so staunchly rejected? With grisly and compelling content anchored in lower-class popular culture and in the context of industrialisation and the growing metropolis, the almost exclusively Victorian genre is closely linked to contemporary social, technological and political developments, which together formed the right context for the creation and the consumption of a popular literature phenomenon that challenged the cultural status quo. Technical advancements such as the introduction of the rotary printing press in England in the 1840s combined with attempts at democratising education from the beginning of the nineteenth century meant that periodical publication was soon considered a promising business opportunity: as a consequence, cheap publications like penny dreadfuls took the burgeoning periodical mass market by storm, reaching astounding circulation numbers as the biggest publishing houses reportedly sold thousands of instalments on a weekly basis.[1] Recent popular culture shows interest by bringing penny dreadfuls back in the limelight through television series, musicals, literature or other forms of popular entertainment, too, though only scratching the surface of the impact of the genre. This study explores different facets of the circulation of penny dreadfuls in their own contemporary context as well as across time and sketches the dynamism and the complexity of this popular fiction genre as key to understanding the penny dreadful's place in the landscape of not only Victorian literature and culture, but also of modern popular entertainment.

The penny dreadful genre flourished in the United Kingdom in the span of only a few decades of existence, already disappearing by the end of the nineteenth century. These sensational stories, sold weekly for the price of one penny, were printed on cheap pulp paper to be sold in mass quantity. Each penny number contained either eight or (more rarely) sixteen pages printed in double columns of text, often including several stories; some were accompanied by a few black and white illustrations. The term 'penny dreadfuls' is accepted as the more general one to encompass serialised, sensationalist, gruesome fiction from the mid-1830s to the end of the 1880s that was primarily marketed to the working-class young, as literacy was increasing significantly in the early Victorian decades. Other phrases tend to be used depending on the publications' precise decade(s), among which 'penny bloods': though sometimes used interchangeably with penny dreadfuls, it in fact designates early penny dreadful publications, often with a more violent tendency, which mostly belong to the period from the mid-1830s until the 1850s. The second half of the century then sees cheap fiction develop and multiply, as penny dreadfuls as well as other formats flood the market for the working-class youth; John Springhall describes that this is when penny fiction became 'appropriated, and in the process transmuted, by a younger age cohort'.[2] This leads to the common designation of 'boys' book', which, though confusingly often used in connection to penny dreadfuls, refers to a cluster of late-Victorian weekly sensational periodicals appearing with the creation of the *Boys of England* magazine and found mostly between the 1870s and the early 1890s.[3] Finally, the 1880s–90s witness the creation of the 'Ha'penny Dreadfuller' by publisher Alfred Harmsworth, which is a crucial step in the history of the penny dreadfuls. As Springhall explains, the 'expansionist 1890s [...] saw a more pronounced racism and imperialism in English popular culture' that led to penny dreadfuls looking more old-fashioned, like 'relics of an era of sensational melodrama' that could not compete with the 'cheaper and more jingoistic' publications such as Harmsworth's.[4] This is why Harmsworth's periodicals *Halfpenny Marvel* (1893–1922) and *Union Jack* (1894–1933) are often considered the end of the penny dreadful.

Penny dreadfuls bear testimony to their historical context as well as to the major shift that occurred in the literary marketplace at the time. The 'unknown public' described by Wilkie Collins in 1858 was a new readership to be reckoned with,[5] not only because of their growing numbers but also because of different needs in terms of entertainment. Rapid industrialisation, urbanisation and the formation of the proletariat were major factors in the consistent development of penny fiction, which E. F. Bleiler summarises in his introduction to the 2008 reedition of *Varney the Vampyre; or, the Feast of Blood* as 'a product of swarming London and the emerging factory metropoles, where enormous masses of semiliterates eagerly read sensational literature'.[6] While novels were still too expensive and too long to plough through for a readership that was not only new to literature but also poor and often only partly literate, penny dreadfuls were the direct answer to the demands of a new market as they were short, cheap stories that the lower classes could afford as well as manage to read entirely, and they included thrilling matters that catered to their readers' sensationalist tastes.

Through suspense, realism, romanticism, Gothic tropes or humour, the serials soon became the most sold type of publication of their time, as hundreds of tales unravelled (some for weeks, others for years), always responding to the market's demands as quickly as the following week. Indeed, this fast-paced publication rhythm was directly dependent on sales numbers: if an issue sold well, there was enough demand to keep the presses printing this precise story. Inevitably, this meant that quantity and speed of delivery superseded quality: the badly edited instalments consistently featured typos, mistakes, sometimes even words printed upside down, and an overall slightly chaotic writing style rife with plot inconsistencies (such as a character famously dying twice in one story). But through these tales, allegedly 'dreadful' in content and in style, literary conventions and characters evolved for a new readership, leading to the creation of expected tropes and techniques that constitute the genre. Understanding the way that society regarded the quality of penny dreadfuls and the revulsion they provoked among the middle and upper classes is, therefore, a valuable tool to analyse the major shift in the production of literature at the time. In the context of the development of the mass market, the penny dreadfuls' successful circulation introduced new criteria for popularity and became a constant challenge to the previous, rather monolithic definition of literature.

Weaponising the Penny Dreadfuls' Successful Circulation

The phrase 'penny dreadfuls' was originally a pejorative label (or 'derogatory' categorisation, as Springhall refers to it in a key study of the penny dreadful's association with criminality) constructed by middle-class journalists in the late-Victorian period as part of the heavily mediatised public war waged against penny fiction and its successful industry throughout the century.[7] In the political context of enfranchisement debates and the rise of Chartism from the end of the 1830s, the higher classes worried about the working class's moral character and how it might impact the political process. The growing number of lower-class readers and cheap publications soon took on a threatening dimension for the hegemony of the bourgeois ruling class, as it made controlling the reading material that was produced increasingly difficult. Penny dreadfuls rapidly came under fire from numerous sources in cyclical, emotionally charged campaigns best described as moral panics: scholars such as Patrick A. Dunae, John Springhall, or more recently Victor Shea, have analysed in detail the social fear of penny publications as heightened by conservative middle-class fears in reaction to contemporary educational reforms (such as the 1870 Forster's Education Act).[8] The communal aspect of reading penny dreadfuls contributed to fears of the lower classes assembling and obtaining more (political) power. In reaction to this, a broad range of publications – scholarly works, pamphlets, political reports, news items – consistently maintained a perspective which discarded this ethically and aesthetically 'wrong' form of literature as unwanted as well as dangerous. This led to penny dreadfuls being either ignored or actively rejected by literary criticism despite their recorded popularity or – considering Michel Foucault's 'rules of exclusion' that regulate any discourse[9] – *because of* their popularity and subversive nature.

While the discourses forming the penny dreadfuls' contemporary criticism include different thematic trends to undermine their weight in society, one unifying strategy emerges: the tendency to weaponise their successful circulation to build a case against them. Easily reaching a consensus on the 'considerable magnitude' of the 'evil',[10] these trends have in common the fact that they justified dismissing penny dreadfuls on the grounds of a large-scale public concern for the greater good, be it in terms of health, education, or morality. One of the main arguments for this exclusion was the poor quality of writing that characterised penny dreadfuls at a time when authors like Charles Dickens or Anthony Trollope produced texts of undeniable literariness according to middle- and upper-class standards. The penny periodicals publishing sensational stories were thus described as a 'mass of literary garbage' requiring 'no intellect' and showing a 'dead level of mediocrity' in numerous pieces both published anonymously and signed by notable authors such as Margaret Oliphant,[11] as they caused dissonance with contemporary attempts at establishing an educational environment aimed at the working classes in the first part of the nineteenth century. Amid the advocacy for the 'spread of cheap, wholesome, good, and attractive books',[12] they were therefore cast as an obstacle to the circulation of a cultural hegemony. However, this supposed lack of educational quality was a misrepresentation of penny periodicals which, in addition to the fiction they included, in fact strove to provide educational material outside of the institutional context as soon as the 1840s.[13] Such discourses epitomise the higher classes' difficulty in accepting major changes that were happening in the literary landscape as well as betray the use of ideological categories in the hopes of gaining control of the newly developing mass market. The same process is at stake when penny dreadfuls are described as 'the plague of poisonous literature':[14] the use of a Gothicised rhetoric of contamination and contagion evokes a form of unwanted and threatening circulation, in this case of metaphorical viruses such as ignorance that must be stopped from spreading by stopping the circulation of the successful publications. Revealing the power dynamics at play, these discourses fashion the growing popular culture into a quasi-Gothic monster that foreshadows social disintegration if left to its own devices, which must therefore be controlled by the higher classes.[15]

The successful circulation of publications that were not disseminated or controlled by the higher classes anymore made tangible fears of a disruption of the social order which manifest in another thematic trend in contemporary criticism: that of the supposed 'inevitable corruption' of penny dreadfuls,[16] i.e. their potential criminal or immoral influence. While the Victorians believed that literature's goal should be to morally educate, the stories of murders, violence, highwaymen and thieves certainly did not have morally virtuous protagonists, and the penny dreadfuls' supposed lack of morality quickly became a key argument for their rejection. A direct causal link was established, as penny dreadfuls were decried as 'socially dangerous' and 'fruitful in [their] supply of candidates for the gaol and the Reformatory'.[17] Penny fiction became directly incriminated in the context of criminal affairs in which newspapers, police reports and juries alike blamed a taste for penny dreadfuls for all sorts of crimes and violent acts, provided that a penny number could be found in the offender's pocket – effectively making them what Springhall calls a 'convenient cultural scapegoat' to avoid questioning the social and economic realities that might have been at the root of such violent acts.[18] Counter-discourses questioning the legitimacy of penny dreadful criticism do emerge at the turn of the century, when writers such as Arthur Quiller-Couch or G. K. Chesterton suggest that it would 'be well to inquire a trifle more deeply into cause and effect'[19] and denounce a propensity to place the blame rapidly in order to avoid reflecting upon the fundamental socio-economic causes that lead to delinquency and criminality. But such discourses remain marginal, and the mainstream view was primarily constituted of attacks on the moral character of the cheap publications.

Beyond discussions of criminality and real-world violence, the connection between penny dreadfuls and immorality was consistently drawn in daily-life contexts, too. Depicted as 'demoralising' their working-class readership,[20] the reading of cheap publications was often assimilated to vices such as alcohol consumption. Penny publications were, for instance, described as 'the natural accompaniment of the gin-glass and the beer-pot'.[21] Drawing on notions of excess, this depicted the working class as unreliable, looking for instant gratification and unable to follow the path deemed acceptable in society. Like in the broader trend of literature of improvement, readers were urged to pursue self-help and so-called rational recreation – i.e. recreation that is 'controlled, ordered, and improving'[22] – in order to be able to seize the opportunities that the industrial society might provide, in a form of patronising guidance aimed at reinforcing the contemporary social order. The dismissal of penny publications as a reprehensible substance to consume bears political implications, too: G. W. M. Reynolds's publications were outspokenly political, and Edward Lloyd's are known to have reported Chartist meetings as well.[23] In this context, the gathering of a reading crowd takes on a new threatening potential, and it becomes even more crucial for middle- and upper-classes to try to guide the crowd back to morality.

The appropriation of literature by the lower classes through these immensely popular and widely circulated publications inscribes itself into what Edward Jacobs calls a 'residually festive, vernacular sub-culture that competed both economically and "morally" with mainstream Victorian culture'.[24] The potential creation of a competing sub-culture, however, activated anxieties about society's future, as its established social order was now under threat of change through rising literacy and changing consumption practices. The threat could not be simply ignored; it had to be eradicated. This active, public rejection of penny dreadfuls is proof of a deep disturbance running through the very core of what formed British middle-class cultural values at the time, in a society conscious of its own changing social and political landscape. Penny dreadfuls were not simply popular: they moved between and connected literary traditions, bringing people together by engaging with their daily lives as well as creating new spaces to learn, discuss, or escape. Culture itself was changing, one penny number at a time; and the urgency of middle- and upper-class attacks on penny dreadfuls and their growing readership reveals a veritable dread of this uncontrollable phenomenon that seems to 'intoxicate' society through its multifaceted circulation.

Recovering the Penny Dreadful in Scholarship

Considering that penny fiction was publicly discarded as aesthetically and ethically 'dreadful', it is hardly surprising to observe that several decades pass before any scholarly attention is bestowed on this genre. This changes only around the mid-twentieth century, when the focus of interest shifts towards the history and culture of the working-class; it is then that E. S. Turner's influential work *Boys Will Be Boys: The Story of Sweeney Todd, Deadwood Dick, Sexton Blake, Billy Bunter, Dick Barton, et al.* (1948) begins to make light of the popular literary culture of the working classes. Literary and cultural studies scholars such as Margaret Dalziel (with *Popular Fiction 100 Years Ago: An Unexplored Tract of Literary History* in 1957) and Richard D. Altick (with *The English Common Reader* in 1957) soon start to investigate the popular fiction that sold millions of copies. The publication of the pioneering *Fiction for the Working-Man 1830–1850: A Study of the Literature Produced for the Working Classes in Early Victorian Urban England* in 1963 by Louis James marks the beginning of an important legitimisation process, coinciding with the rise of Marxist historiography and scholarly endeavours such as the History Workshop Movement or the foundation of the Birmingham School of Cultural Studies in 1964, when scholars like Raymond Williams or E. P. Thompson turn to a systematic engagement with 'history from below'.[25]

The body of scholarly work produced from the mid-1950s to the present sheds light on the historical, social and cultural circumstances of penny dreadfuls, insisting on their significance for the Victorian entertainment industry and the growth of literacy alike. These aspects are crucial: by breaking new ground, such publications helped secure the place of penny dreadfuls as potential objects of study. A few key studies later succeeded in establishing a more specific analytical focus: John Springhall (1994), for instance, addresses penny dreadful publications as cultural turning points in the Victorian landscape, following Louis James's work; others such as Anne Humpherys (1983; 1990) or Ian Haywood (2003) have written fundamental scholarly discussions of these serial works of fiction, as reacting to popular politics and responding to the rise of radicalism, or as 'a new kind of popular literature with radical credentials',[26] respectively. Crucial referencing work has also been performed over the past three decades, which has led to a more accurate scholarly understanding of the popular phenomenon of penny fiction thanks to Elizabeth James and Helen R. Smith's cataloguing of the British Library's Barry Ono Collection of Victorian cheap serialised fiction in *Penny Dreadfuls and Boy's Adventures* (1998) or, more recently, Marie Léger-St-Jean's *Price One Penny: A Database of Cheap Literature, 1837–1860* (2010), an online catalogue of early Victorian penny fiction which gathers bibliographic information and provides statistical input after considerable archival research.

Building on the studies that have provided key contexts for understanding penny bloods and penny dreadfuls in the light of their literary and cultural background, the past decade has shown decided interest in challenging the notion of literary canon, as Daragh Downes and Trish Ferguson problematise in their critical study *Victorian Fiction Beyond the Canon* (2016). In it, they return to Walter Pater's aestheticist reconceptualization of criticism, which 'advocated moving away from […] a consensus about what was "best worth reading", in an increasingly diversified literary marketplace' and thus contrast with

Matthew Arnold's cultural hierarchy, pointing out the obvious starting-point as 'to seek out those books with enjoyed great popularity during the era but have since lost favour and fallen out of circulation'.[27] In this spirit, full-length studies of the penny dreadful as literary object and/or of precise authors or publishers have recently multiplied, demonstrating the topicality but also the necessity of such research in a wider investigation of popular entertainment. Sarah Louise Lill and Rohan McWilliam's *Edward Lloyd and His World: Popular Fiction, Politics and the Press in Victorian Britain* (2019) is a long-overdue study of a key publisher of penny fiction, who they convincingly argue must be 'reclaimed as an eminent Victorian'.[28] That same year, Anna Gasperini's *Nineteenth Century Popular Fiction, Medicine and Anatomy: The Victorian Penny Blood and the 1832 Anatomy Act* (2019) was the first monograph performing a cross-sectional literary analysis of selected penny blood texts. Other key contributions to the field build on one another: Jennifer Conary and Mary L. Shannon's collection *G. W. M. Reynolds Reimagined: Studies in Authorship, Radicalism, and Genre, 1830–1870* (2023) is a welcome expansion of Louis James and Anne Humpherys's *G. W. M. Reynolds: Nineteenth-Century Fiction, Politics, and the Press* (2008), Shannon's own *Dickens, Reynolds, and Mayhew on Wellington Street: The Print Culture of a Victorian Street* (2015), and Stephen Knight's *G. W. M. Reynolds and His Fiction: The Man Who Outsold Dickens* (2018) through a consistent focus on the best-selling publisher. Nicole C. Dittmer and Sophie Raine's *Penny Dreadfuls and the Gothic: Investigations of Pernicious Tales of Terror* (2023) is the first collection dedicated exclusively to the literary analysis of a variety of more or less forgotten penny dreadfuls through one common thematic lens; Rebecca Nesvet's *James Malcolm Rymer, Penny Fiction, and the Family* (2025) chooses to place the focus on a prolific but overlooked writer, who authored some of the most famous penny works with the stories of Sweeney Todd and Varney the Vampyre. *Penny Dreadfuls: The Circulation Patterns of a Victorian Popular Genre* is therefore anchored in a very prolific scholarly conversation, but it adopts a more transversal approach. Instead of choosing to select a particular thematic focus, this book hinges on the concept of circulation to present a comprehensive exploration of penny dreadfuls and penny bloods as popular fiction texts, in their contemporary literary and cultural context as well as through their resonances into the present day.

Circulation as a Conceptual Tool

The notion of circulation, which in a publishing context expresses successful dissemination, allows for a productive analysis of the penny dreadfuls' specific nature, role and function as a popular fiction genre. The nineteenth-century popular press had a significantly dynamic character, as Laurel

Brake skilfully summarises in her contribution to *The Routledge Handbook to Nineteenth-Century British Periodicals and Newspapers* (2016);[29] understanding circulation as a broader concept than as only connected to sales numbers is therefore particularly fruitful here. In sum, circulation is primarily concerned with motion: to circulate is to be dynamic, in constant movement, which is especially topical in the Victorian periodical publishing environment. As a concept, circulation is often connected with consumption, which makes sense in this context of shifting economic practices and the development of the mass market. In Marxist terms, circulation is the defining feature of capital: every capital is circulating capital and operates within an expanding circle which creates value.[30] Though penny dreadfuls did indeed circulate as commodities, sold for a profit, their mode of consumption already resists the functioning of their capitalist society: a large proportion of the readership in fact did not participate in the marketplace and thus did *not* generate the desired surplus value. This connects directly to Michael Warner's theory in his study of public address that the circulation of texts is what gathers people and creates a social space, or a public.[31] As objects, penny dreadfuls are thus already connected to established definitions of the economic and the social dimensions of circulation; but the concept is also tied to their history, content, movements and rejection. Hence the title of this introduction: there is circulation *of* the penny dreadfuls, but also *in* the penny dreadfuls.

Tracing the different patterns of circulation of penny dreadfuls beyond the mere expression of sales numbers is an ideal way to understand their dynamics and their complexity as a literary and a cultural phenomenon. The periodicals themselves circulated through the city and its communities, fostering a new social spirit of gathering and satisfying a growing readership's morbid tastes, while at the same time, other parts of society were trying to stop their physical and metaphorical circulation to limit their impact. Meanwhile, penny dreadfuls circulated between literary genres, and the stories themselves, like their own criticism, were filled to the brim with metaphors and discourses of circulation as desired, purposeful, silent, despised, unwanted or feared. In his monograph *The Social Life of Fluids: Blood, Milk, and Water in the Victorian Novel* (2010), Jules Law engages with the interaction of the literal and the figurative dimensions of circulation, as he persuasively outlines circulation as one of the central mediums of expression for Victorian anxieties about subjectivity and the social body. In this spirit, I contend that the concept of circulation captures the social, temporal, spatial and economic dimensions of the penny dreadfuls' nature and context; and the constant intersection of these dimensions reveals what disturbed the higher social strata enough to have penny dreadfuls outright rejected, that is, as far as form, literary content, lack of object value or readership were concerned.

Through the concept of circulation, I examine the penny dreadfuls' nature, function and movements in their contemporary literary and cultural context(s) and beyond. The penny dreadfuls' dynamism is key, as they challenge generic classification, the unsettled nature of which Andrew King, Alexis Easley and John Morton raise in *The Routledge Handbook to Nineteenth-Century British Periodicals and Newspapers* (2016).[32] This book uses circulation as a concept to examine both the life and the afterlife of penny dreadfuls, that is, their impact on later popular literature and entertainment and the circulation of their features in neo-Victorian narratives. Thwarting their contemporary society's striving for order, penny dreadfuls circulated representations of crimes throughout communities, seeming to revel in proving social anxieties about cleanliness justified. Their diachronic circulation proves that penny dreadfuls remained dynamic and fluid material across time, too. That is why the concept underpins this entire exploration of the influential Victorian popular genre, as I argue that circulation allows us not only to situate penny dreadfuls in relation to contemporary reading and publishing practices, but also to reappraise the complexity of penny dreadfuls and to trace the relationship they have with the constitution of societal relationships and with the popular.

Tracing Circulation Patterns

To explore penny dreadfuls as a Victorian popular genre through their patterns of circulation, this study focuses on specific penny blood examples from texts published in the 1840s that are known to have been among the most sold and/or circulated at the time. While the penny dreadful phenomenon continues and evolves throughout the Victorian period, the 1840s constitute their first full decade of existence through penny bloods, and it is then that they experiment and establish their fluidity and their malleability. A focus on the time-period preceding the rise of the sensation novel allows an investigation of penny bloods before the expansion of the market, too: by the 1850s, a significant shift in popular literature occurs as genres and themes multiply, the more unified body of publications referred to as penny bloods disappears, and penny dreadfuls begin to metamorphose to become more associated with adventure and fantasy. The patterns of circulation that are traced in this study originate before this dilution of the penny fiction market and are therefore best exemplified through texts such as G. W. M. Reynolds's or Edward Lloyd's, household names of the penny publishing industry.[33] Reynolds himself was hailed in his obituary as the 'most popular writer of his time', his body of work outselling Charles Dickens's,[34] and Lloyd 'changed the face of popular publishing for generations to come'.[35]

Their most widely distributed texts were published within a very short time – the first series of *The Mysteries of London* (1844–1845), *Varney the Vampyre; or, the Feast of Blood* (1845–1847) and *The String of Pearls: A Romance* (1846–1847) – and encapsulate the early patterns of circulation that participate in the creation and consumption of this Victorian popular genre. In this study, I demonstrate that these patterns are undoubtedly what allowed the penny dreadful genre to firmly establish itself as a cornerstone of popular culture and to thrive and remain dynamic across the entire Victorian period and beyond.

The chapters constituting this book consider the penny dreadfuls' multifaceted circulation and explore their dialogue with their contemporary society through the cultural, social and political tensions they problematise: the way they behave(d) within the literary marketplace; their relationship with other literary genres and traditions of the popular; their impact on later popular culture, all the way to the twenty-first century. In the same way that their circulation forms a spiral-like pattern, always touching back to specific points but always moving forward, this study connects key elements and patterns of the publications and the texts they contain, locating them within existing conversations while at the same time broadening the conversation to which they give rise. Through the lens of the concept of circulation which pervades their history and content, this book reassesses the impact of the penny dreadful on nineteenth-century print culture and entertainment as well as on contemporary popular culture, and demonstrates the importance of this Victorian popular genre to better understand broader notions of popular culture and to keep deconstructing such binaries as 'high' and 'low' culture. In so doing, it also reveals how the penny dreadfuls' material aspect is intimately interwoven with their seriality, their cultural significance, the reactions they provoked and their actual content. The resulting picture informs us about the nineteenth century's social history and culture, about class warfare and political change, and about the evolution of literature over the past two hundred and fifty years. In the end, the analysis of this circulation should help us do just what was suggested in the popular satirical magazine *Punch, or the London Charivari* in 1895, quoted in the epigraph of this introduction: let us 'endeavour […] to be *just* to the poor "Penny Dreadful"'[36] and let us explore its rich and complex life and afterlife.

Notes

1 Neuburg, *Popular Literature*, 157; James, *Fiction for the Working Man*, 41.
2 Springhall, 'Disseminating', 568.
3 Over the years, penny dreadfuls have mistakenly been referred to as boys' books, therefore creating a bias in the representation of the penny dreadfuls' readership. Because of this, the readership was long assumed to be restricted to boys and young

men, and penny dreadfuls were consequently labelled as connected to immaturity and masculinity, reinforcing gender stereotypes and painting a simplistic picture. However, recent scholarship and recovered testimonies of booksellers confirm that customers of penny dreadfuls were of all ages and genders (see for instance Rose 1995).

4 Ibid., 577.
5 Collins, 'Unknown Public', 217.
6 Bleiler, 'Introduction', 785.
7 Springhall, 'Pernicious Reading', 326.
8 Dunae, 'Penny Dreadfuls', 150; Springhall, 'Pernicious Reading', 326; Shea, 'Penny Dreadfuls', 185–186.
9 Foucault, 'Order of Discourse', 1461.
10 The London Hermit, 'Physiology of Penny Awfuls', 376.
11 Oliphant, 'Byways of Literature', 360; 'Mischievous Literature', 446.
12 'Mischievous Literature', 448.
13 See Burz-Labrande 2021.
14 Greenwood, 'Short Way to Newgate', 158.
15 Burz-Labrande, 'Embalmed Pestilence', 91–113.
16 Dixon, 'Literature of the Lower Orders', 3.
17 Hollingsworth, *Newgate Novel*, 15; 'What Boys Read', 96.
18 Springhall, 'Pernicious Reading', 327.
19 Quiller-Couch, 'Poor Little Penny Dreadful', 278; see also Chesterton 1901.
20 Phillips Day, *Juvenile Crime*, 203.
21 Meteyard, 'Cheap Literature', 220.
22 Cunningham, *Leisure*, 90.
23 Haywood, *Revolution*, 162–170.
24 Jacobs, 'Disvaluing the Popular', 90.
25 The phrase 'history from below' was already used previously, for instance by Lucien Febvre in 1932 or by A. L. Morton in his 1938 work *A People's History of England*, but E. P. Thompson's 1966 essay 'History from Below' is what truly made the phrase a staple of these new historiographic currents.
26 Haywood, *Revolution*, 162.
27 Downes and Ferguson, *Victorian Fiction*, 2, 3.
28 Lill and McWilliam, *Edward Lloyd*, 3.
29 Brake, 'Markets', 243.
30 Marx, 'Grundrisse', ch. 12; *Capital*, ch. 4.
31 Warner, 'Publics and Counterpublics', 420.
32 King, Easley and Morton, 'Introduction', 9.
33 For more on the consensus reached by Victorianist scholars of popular literature on the two publishers' popularity, see for instance James 1963; Neuburg 1977; Haywood 2003; Humpherys and James 2008; Shannon 2015; Knight 2018; Gasperini 2019; Lill and McWilliam 2019; Conary and Shannon 2023.
34 'G. W. M. Reynolds', 600; see also Knight 2018.
35 Lill and McWilliam, *Edward Lloyd*, 10.
36 'That Poor Penny Dreadful', 109, emphasis original.

Chapter 1
FROM ORAL STORYTELLING TO SERIALITY

Defining the popularity of a cheap nineteenth-century publication with accuracy can be an arduous task, verging on impossible due to the scarcity of information available to the modern reader. Although some numbers are available thanks to publisher records or other informative sources, these records were not always made public and might not have been preserved for posterity. Editorials or publisher statements cannot be considered a reliable source either, as the numbers they boasted were often a more accurate representation of their marketing skills than of actual sales. Circulation numbers, as established from a publisher's sales numbers, are therefore not representative enough: even when available, they only record one sale to one customer, freezing it in time as if this were the final leg of the instalment's journey. Yet this was not the last step in a publication's life. Whether it was a so-called triple-decker novel, a pamphlet or a penny blood publication, any work would continue moving further through communities after its first sale; with the help of circulating libraries, for more expensive middle-class works, or simply travelling from hand to hand, for cheap publications that targeted the working class. In short, even documented sales numbers can only ever represent a portion of the actual community of readers who engaged with the work, and an important proportion of the reading public can be assumed to not have had an active part as buyer in the literary marketplace.

Communal Readings and Shared Experience

In the case of penny bloods and dreadfuls, communal readings as documented by various sources (either contemporary to their time of publication or in the following decades) are key to understanding the reading experience they provided. Following Jonathan Rose's suggestion that it is necessary to turn to the readers rather than draw conclusions from the texts alone, since the latter will lead to what he defines as 'receptive fallacy',[1] the first step to understanding the popularity of cheap fiction is to turn to testimonies provided by investigative journalism as well as working-class autobiographies. Margaret Willes points out that autobiographies of working men and women, though they already developed in the eighteenth century, became a more established genre around the very beginning of the nineteenth century, and she describes how a number of them 'relate how reading liberated them'.[2] Descriptions in autobiographies of their subject's own reading experiences are surprisingly numerous, and like Henry Mayhew's accounts *London Labour and the London Poor* (1851), they regularly mention various forms of collective reading of penny bloods and show a strong link to the tradition of oral storytelling, perpetuating the circulation of penny bloods orally instead of only physically.

According to numerous contemporary testimonies, people would tend to gather and listen to someone reading out a penny story at the end of the working day. The reader might be someone who was able to afford the latest instalment, but more importantly, they would likely have a relatively good level of literacy; the listeners would, for the most part, be those unable to buy and/or to read but interested in the stories. In the first volume of his account, Mayhew describes costermongers who 'were able to read, or loved to listen to reading' and points to the 'excitement derived from hearing stories read' as a staple of working-class experience.[3] Emphasising a love for oral storytelling, this also points towards the fact that not all costermongers could read well or at all: a great number of working-class people at the time were indeed just partly literate, able to engage with written words to a certain degree only. Additionally, if some of them were able to decipher a periodical and slowly make their way through the story, the painstaking effort required can be assumed to have left virtually no room for 'excitement', whereas hearing the story read out by someone more literate would have allowed them to become engrossed in it. The section titled 'The Literature of Costermongers' in Mayhew's first volume addresses these communal readings most extensively:

> It may appear anomalous to speak of the literature of an uneducated body, but even the costermongers have their tastes for books. They are very fond of hearing any one read aloud to them, and listen very attentively. One man often reads the Sunday paper of the beer-shop to them, and on a fine summer's evening a costermonger, or any neighbour who has the advantage of being 'a schollard', reads aloud to them in the courts they inhabit. What they love best to listen to – and, indeed, what they are most eager for – are Reynolds's periodicals [...].[4]

This excerpt showcases the popularity of such stories as penny bloods by referring to G. W. M. Reynolds's periodicals and hints at an audience much broader than the number of actual buyers suggests. Mayhew's description does bear a moralising tone in parts: starting with an upper-class incredulity about the 'anomalous' idea that 'even the costermongers' have an interest in literature, despite being an 'uneducated body', it also uses a quasi-mocking tone to report working-class speech. By quoting how someone who can read is called a 'schollard' by their neighbours, Mayhew reproduces on the page a mispronunciation of the word 'scholar', choosing to visually signal the lack of education of the person who is quoted and investing the juxtaposed phrase 'who has the advantage of' with irony. Despite the class-based judgement that transpires here, Mayhew's account establishes a clear link between penny bloods and oral storytelling, as aurality is emphasised: 'hearing', 'aloud', 'listen' and 'read to' are repeated throughout the description of these shared moments and take precedence over the mentions of what was actually read. The prevailing notion is that this so-called 'uneducated body [...] are very fond of hearing any one read aloud to them' and of sharing the excitement and the thrill of fiction, regardless of their (non-)education.

While allowing the contemporary social hierarchy to show through, Mayhew's work remains a ground-breaking and extremely informative account of previously ignored working-class experiences. The 'Literature of the Costermongers' section contains more instances of communal readings: 'They had assembled, after their day's work or their rounds, for the purpose of hearing my informant read the last number of some of the penny publications', the 'informant' being an 'intelligent costermonger, who had recently read some of the cheap periodicals to ten or twelve men, women, and boys, all costermongers'.[5] The diversity of the hearing public (and thus indirectly reading public) is here brought to light along with the eagerness provoked by these publications, which justified assembling after an undoubtedly long day of work in order to hear 'the last number'. Such eagerness is also obvious in a further comment this informant offers, which also stresses the collaborative nature of the reading experience: 'I have known a man, what couldn't read, buy a periodical what had an illustration, a little out of the common way perhaps, just that he might learn from someone, who *could* read, what it was all about'.[6] As Mayhew's further investigation shows, this enthusiasm was also not limited to costermongers and working people in general: his third volume contains a section about 'London Vagrants', which mentions William Ainsworth's Newgate Novel *Jack Sheppard* (1839–1840) as 'borrowed from the circulating library, and read aloud in the low lodging-houses in the evening by those who have a little education, to their companions who have none'.[7] If he then goes on to deplore the 'baneful' effect of such literature, which he describes as 'guilty of pandering to the most depraved propensities',[8] thus locating himself within the currents of criticism that connected cheap fiction with criminality, the mention of group readings of such tales confirms a successful circulation in the tradition of oral storytelling across a wide range of social groups. Mayhew's reports have since been critically analysed and confirmed by numerous book history and social history scholars, such as Margaret Willes in *Reading Matters: Five Centuries of Discovering Books* (2008), in which she accordingly concludes that 'those who could neither read nor write could enjoy the pleasures of literature by being read to'.[9] The sensationalist penny publications were, therefore, selling to the literate and the illiterate, bringing lower-class people together in sharing resources (one can buy, another one can read) to experience the excitement of literature as a group.

Literacy and Consumption of Literature

To clarify why penny blood fiction and other cheap publications were so popular and consumed in such a communal form, examining the period's socio-economic circumstances is crucial, as this resurgence of an oral storytelling tradition is intrinsically linked to a gradual change in the mode of consumption of literature aligned with contemporary living conditions of the working-class. I prefer not to use the phrase 'common reader', which Richard D. Altick favours in *The English Common Reader* (1957), the first comprehensive exploration of the social history of the mass reading public in England. Although Altick's work is immensely valuable as one of the pioneering studies that made research on popular fiction possible, I will rather discuss what Margaret Willes defines as a 'readership constrained by economic factors'[10] and focus on either 'working-class readers' or the 'reading public' in general. The term of 'common reader', while helpful at the time, proves to be too much of a 'catch-all description of a group that is far from homogeneous',[11] as it encompassed various social and economic conditions in a study focused on the expansion of print culture and on book history more than on readership. In his foreword to the second edition of *The English Common Reader* (1998), Jonathan Rose explains the debt we owe to Altick's work while also pointing out that 'since then [...], we have recovered the primary sources that Altick lacked: the memoirs and diaries of ordinary people, school records, library borrowing registers, marginalia, social surveys, oral interviews, letters to the editor'.[12] These advances in social history allow scholars to try to 'fill in the white spaces on Altick's outline map'.[13] In the following, I trace the links between the oral experience of penny blood fiction and the changing conditions of the consumption of literature for the working-class in order to help 'fill in' this map of the reading public.

The issue of literacy in the nineteenth century is a long-discussed one, and ongoing research regularly brings to light new information, often requiring estimates to be adjusted. For instance, Willes points out that literacy percentages had to be reviewed after it was demonstrated that a person could use an X as a signature without it automatically accounting for illiteracy.[14] By the middle of the century, the proportion of illiterate men across the country is gauged to be around forty per cent, and that of illiterate women as slightly higher.[15] In addition to this, by 1861, the population was estimated at about twenty million, nine of which were eighteen years old or younger, which means that forty-five per cent of the potential reading public were children.[16] The period of the penny bloods is also pre-Forster's Education Act, which was passed in 1870 and sought to provide *all* children from the age of five – regardless of their background or class – with a rudimentary education. Although such a legal framework does not necessarily guarantee a higher literacy rate later in the century, these numbers do provide a picture of how much of the population was unable to read or write at the time of the penny bloods' publication, which is consistent with a mode of reading that necessitates a communal aspect and allows a shared experience.

Furthermore, the contemporary educational structures put into place before Forster's Education Act very much lend themselves to a Foucauldian reading of schooling as discipline. Edward Jacobs explains that during the nineteenth century's early decades, the regime of popular education put in place by initiatives such as Andrew Bell's National Society for the Education of the Poor in the Principles of the Established Church (established in 1811) or the British and Foreign School Society for the Education of the Labouring and Manufacturing Classes of Society of Every Religious Persuasion (1814, developed from Joseph Lancaster's School formed in 1798) 'constructed literacy as a mechanical discipline very much like factory production'.[17] Early schools relied on strict methods of reproduction, imitation and memorisation which, Jacobs argues, were at odds with the orality and liveliness of street culture.[18] They also worked with a system of rewards for 'acceptable reproduction of the models' consisting in 'power over other students',[19] thereby using the double system described in Michel Foucault's *Discipline and Punish* as 'gratification-punishment'.[20] The rigor ruling this pedagogical model can be described, with Foucault, as 'moral orthopaedics', in that this schooling 'facilitated the production and circulation of knowledge amongst bodies under controlled conditions'.[21] A parallel can also be drawn with the contemporary rise of industrialism, as children and adults become part of what Foucault calls the 'production apparatus'; not to be understood merely in an economic sense as Roger Deacon points out,[22] but 'also [as] the production of knowledge and skills in the school'.[23] Along with these characteristics, 'disciplinary time [...] gradually imposed on pedagogical practice'[24] in an increasingly institutionalised schooling of the poor also participated in the creation of 'an underclass whose experiences had taught them to resent and mistrust the culture represented by industrial work and schooled literacy'.[25] Because of this resentment, one might speculate, the lower classes turned towards material such as penny publications, which were closer to the oral, festive street culture that Jacobs describes. In addition to the educational potential of cheap periodical instalments such as the ones published by Edward Lloyd, which I have analysed elsewhere,[26] penny blood fiction became a motivating medium for education and literacy. Working-class autobiographers confirm this tendency in several contemporary testimonies which suggest that penny fiction was not only entertainment but also reading practice as well as a form of education. Rose emphasises the common occurrence of such statements as Alfred Cox's 'I trace [my budding love of literature] to an enthusiastic reading of Penny Dreadfuls which, so far from leading me into a life of crime, made me look for something better' in autobiographies,[27] which demonstrate that contrary to the upper-class dread that penny fiction would turn the lower class into criminals, it actually was often a form of 'improvement' (to reuse contemporary vocabulary) for its readers.

Becoming part of the cheap fiction readership as an audience member rather than an actual reader also reflected an economic necessity. Regardless of one's literacy, hearing a story instead of reading it was much more suited to the financial reality of most of the lower-class, who could not always afford to buy an instalment, never mind on a weekly basis. Preserving the link to this oral tradition therefore ties in with a new mode of consumption suited to the contemporary living conditions and financial realities. Of course, the very format of penny fiction already attested to a market evolution aimed at permitting the lower classes to become consumers too: early nineteenth-century three-volume novels typically cost a guinea and a half in the 1820s, which translated as a week's worth of earnings for a skilled London artisan,[28] and which was the equivalent of thirty-one shillings and a half or 378 pence at the time. From 1836 and starting with the *Pickwick Papers*, Charles Dickens's serialised publications were already revolutionary, providing shorter reading material at the price of only one shilling per instalment – but this still meant twelve times the price of penny fiction. In an extensive study published in 1900, A. L. Bowley presents the average of weekly wages for *all* workers nationwide as being around fourteen to fifteen shillings.[29] At a time when costermongers in London earned between ten and thirty shillings a week, carpenters less than seven shillings and common labourers less than four,[30] and given that 'professions' such as toshers (who scavenged in the sewers), mudlarkers (who searched the river shores for items to resell) and pure-finders (who collected dog faeces to sell to tanneries) were rife among the lower classes, spending a shilling to read was not within everyone's reach.

This meant that lower-class readers developed a more practical relationship with literature than higher classes had done, by necessity. Communal readings ensured that one penny spent brought the story to several listeners, which was a much more economical mode of consumption, regardless of whether one could read. What is more, there are testimonies of these publications continuing their circulation through poor communities as useful, practical items once they had been read – in a word, recycling in its early days. Janice Carlisle describes that 'leaves from books and periodicals of all description were used [by costermongers] to wrap meat, fish, sweets, and tobacco, as well as cheese',[31] relying on Mayhew's section on 'street-buyers of waste (paper)' in volume two of *London Labour and the London Poor*. In it, one of Mayhew's informants states that 'his wife schemed to go to the shops who "wrapped up their things from books", in order that he might have something to read after his day's work',[32] and although it concerns a broad range of publications in this precise case, the statement echoes the following comment from volume one found in the 'Literature of the Costermongers' section:

> From other quarters I learned that some of the costermongers who were able to read, or loved to listen to reading, purchased their literature in a very commercial spirit, frequently buying the periodical which is the largest in size, because when 'they've got the reading out of it', as they say, 'it's worth a halfpenny for the barrow'.[33]

The mention of 'commercial spirit' by Mayhew might have been another mark of upper-class condescension, yet it is an accurate interpretation. Here, this so-called 'commercial spirit' is marked by the ability to consider the different uses of the purchase and optimise a spending. The fiction contained within the periodical is not the only point of interest, as the second life of the purchased paper matters, too: this commercial spirit considers the remaining value of the investment once 'they've got the reading out of it', i.e., how the page could be used once emptied of its novelty and entertainment aspect. By making the best that they could out of their available resources, these costermongers were part of the development of a new mode of consumption of literature, using it not only for its content but for its materiality, too. Through reusing and recycling periodicals, they became active agents in the circulation of the material through society – and given the example found in Mayhew's second volume, penny literature still had the potential to go from reading material to wrapper to reading material again, coming full circle.

Relying on the power of orality to expand the penny bloods' readership helped bring about a shift for more availability of literature in society, as its circulation became facilitated by its readers, not merely the marketplace.

The potential sense of community revolving around this new element surely participated in the reasons why such texts disturbed the higher spheres so much and needed to be so categorically rejected. Sensationalist fiction provided the creation of a new cultural memory and shared experience through social gatherings organised *by* the lower classes *for* the lower classes, and Michael Diamond hints at the lasting impact of this aspect:

> Although these sensations were ephemeral, in that their time was soon past, they had an afterlife beyond the weeks, months, or even years during which they held the public in thrall. [...] They provided a common experience [...] something to talk about.[34]

The working-class acquired a threatening potential through such 'common experience' that gave them 'something to talk about' that was out of the upper classes' control; and gatherings of people belonging to the class that was the largest in number, forming groups around material that was not pre-validated by hegemonic discourse, directly feed into Matthew Arnold's fear of anarchy in society. In his series of essays published as *Culture and Anarchy* (1867–1869), Arnold argues that culture 'is, or ought to be, the study and pursuit of perfection',[35] and favours an elevated and high-minded society relying on the State in the hopes of countering the vulgarity and personal freedom that would, in his view, lead to anarchy. If he believed in a collective movement towards culture as perfection, it was certainly a movement spurred by the higher classes, and working-class groups gathering to read discredited publications in spite of the upper classes' injunctions to 'improve' represent the freedom that Arnold believed would lead to anarchy.

The gatherings of working-class groups to read such publicly admonished texts justify Arnold's fears of potential anarchy further as the readers' interests shift towards fiction concerned with their contemporary institutions and with the political. Mayhew documents this change as follows:

> What they love best to listen to – and, indeed, what they are most eager for – are Reynolds's periodicals, especially the 'Mysteries of the Court'. 'They've got tired of Lloyd's blood-stained stories', said one man, who was in the habit of reading to them, 'and I'm satisfied that, of all London, Reynolds is the most popular man among them'.[36]

Bearing in mind that Mayhew's investigative work was published in 1851, this quotation addresses a change in the tastes of penny fiction readership: Lloyd's penny bloods correspond to the early to mid-1840s, whereas Reynolds's famous *Mysteries of London* (1844–1845) were quickly followed by his *Mysteries of the Court of London*, which would run from 1848 to 1856. Mayhew goes on to state that

> The tales of robbery and bloodshed, of heroic, eloquent, and gentlemanly highwaymen, or of gipsies turning out to be nobles, now interest the costermongers but little, although they found great delight in such stories a few years back. Works relating to Courts, potentates, or 'harristocrats', are the most relished by these rude people.[37]

The direct quotation of the mispronunciation of the word 'aristocrat' shows that Mayhew intentionally associates the Cockney dialect – after all, 'it is the unhappy slippery h which is of all other failings that most commonly associated with Cockneyisms'[38] – with supposedly 'rude' (in the sense of uneducated, ignorant) people, which epitomises the power struggle at play in the popularity of penny publications among the masses. This quotation addresses an interest shift towards more immediately relevant penny fiction that deals with the people in power or the institutions that surround them; Reynolds was also famously a Chartist, his fiction often dealing with politics and power.[39] The lower-class readership therefore showed more political interest than before, which gives even more power (both symbolically and literally) to the social gatherings organised around the reading of penny bloods. Consequently, it became all the more urgent to attempt to contain the phenomenon and to discredit both the publications and their readers, as Mayhew does here. Using the Cockney dialect of the speaker to denigrate the reading tastes of 'these rude people' is, however, counter-productive: Cockney was the 'language of the major portion of the great city's inhabitants',[40] which lends even more power to the expressed opinion by suggesting it is widely circulated. Combined with the turn towards more directly pertinent penny fiction concerned with political power and institutions, this adds to the symbolic power of the lower-class readership gathered around the reading of penny bloods. What is more, the fact that such publications remain strongly anchored in the oral storytelling tradition through the mode of consumption established by readers themselves accelerates the potential circulation of knowledge and of information through the lower spheres of society. At the end of the eighteenth century, Reverend Dr John Trusler feared that the spread of printing and of the press in England would provoke a similar political upheaval to that in France, and stated that he was 'bold to say that the more untaught the labouring part of mankind are, the more humble are they and modest and the better servants they make'.[41] This fear seems to be echoed by the penny bloods' circulation fostering community through its oral dimension, and is then reverberated in the fear of anarchy present in Arnold's essays a few decades later.

Seriality as a Writing and a Consumption Practice

The development of a new mass readership led to changing conditions of consumption, and therefore to new modes of publishing and of writing in order to adapt to a new target audience. This explains the transition to seriality that took the literary marketplace by storm from the 1830s onwards. Serialisation is, in fact, a 'crucial factor in understanding the way Victorian literary culture worked',[42] and seriality as a mode is indeed 'closely intertwined with the debate over the role and function of mass culture'.[43] With the beginning of a mass market economy, the living circumstances previously addressed meant that the potential readership did not have either enough time, enough money or enough literacy to dedicate itself to a full volume such as those traditionally published until then. To become successful among the masses, literature had to be delivered in a format that could be folded, carried in pockets and read whenever the opportunity arose, and serial literature thus personified a view of life that was 'intrinsic to Victorian culture'[44] – a claim clearly substantiated by the colossal amount of serial fiction published in the nineteenth century as well as by studies of serialisation in the Victorian era.[45]

Serialisation as a publishing practice indicates a significantly different approach to literature as a whole, as it marks a strong departure from the consumption practices of the novel. Indeed, it was not only tied to the mode of production and writing of literature: the notion of seriality is equally relevant in terms of reception of the material, i.e. how it was read.[46] The growing practice of serialisation impacted the consumption of literature, as it reimagined and redefined its definition. Stephen Colclough opens his 2007 study *Consuming Texts* by quoting the Venetian nobleman Pococurante from Voltaire's *Candide* (1759), who shows his impressive library to Candide and says of a precious edition of Homer that 'you had to have it in your library, like an ancient monument, or like those rusty medals that have no commercial value'.[47] The novel, which was as much a literary story as it was an item that belonged on a shelf and within the closed space of the domestic sphere, was therefore consumed in a vastly different way from popular penny literature: the acquisition of a book was also the acquisition of a commodity to reflect cultural capital. If Victorian three-volume novels, or triple-deckers, did mark a crucial stage in the cultural democratisation of the novel and its development as popular literature, their format still meant that the book object was to be taken care of, all the more so since this form of publishing relied heavily on the system of circulating libraries where it would need to be returned. Reading thus acquired a different status through the rise of periodical fiction, as the marketplace did not depend exclusively on books that should be displayed side by side like medals on a shelf but evolved to provide a more mass-reading, working-class appropriate format thanks to the use of seriality in cheap, short numbers.

Connected to the move away from consumption practices such as that of the novel, another aspect of serial literature that made it perhaps suspicious in the eyes of the upper classes is that this radically new approach towards literature also questioned the status of authorship. A vast number of penny bloods were published anonymously, sometimes using formulations such as 'by the author of [...]' as a marketing technique but often omitting the name of the author. Through this, these publications disturbed the Romantic notion of the author as a 'unique individual uniquely responsible for a unique product'[48] and signalled a move away from the 'Romantic concern with individual creation and responsibility to a Victorian stress on narrative integration'.[49] Rather than preserving the image of a solitary genius creating his work, serial fiction 'confuted the "catastrophic" notion of artistic inspiration, a kind of gigantic creative shudder that results in a single aesthetic product'.[50] This destabilisation came both from serialisation, and therefore expansion of reading time, and from the fact that an anonymous publication could be the work of a famous literary genius just as it could be – and often was – several authors working one after the other. The Romantic mental picture of reading was also destabilised, as reading now could belong to a group of working men listening to a tale at night and in a dirty London street, as much as it belonged to a nobleman in the safety of his private library. These new contexts and the evolution of the corresponding material thus led to the appropriation of notions that previously belonged to another sphere, and it is surely the growing porousness of spheres and the potential threat of invasion and 'contamination' that engendered such an important backlash and such targeted discourses from the upper classes as the ones I have analysed elsewhere.[51]

In terms of storytelling techniques, seriality in a nineteenth-century context answered the readership's circumstances by shifting the focus towards one individual instalment rather than on the completion of a narrative. This different attitude towards fiction, and towards the act of reading in general, impacted the writing process as well, in that seriality became a tool which helped literary genres evolve to adapt to the new mode of consumption of literature. The fast-paced publication rhythm of weekly penny numbers consequently allowed as well as required experimentation with writing, in order to keep up with the readership's new interests and habits. More than a mere economic strategy, serialisation was 'a literary form attuned to fundamental tendencies in the age at large', one of the most crucial ones being that 'reading did not occur in an enclosed realm of contemplation [but rather] much more within the busy context of everyday life. It was not possible to enter into an imaginary world and remain there until the story's end'.[52]

The growing access to consumption gained by the lower classes involved a different approach towards time and towards the structure of a day. As Willes remarks, factory workers toiled away at monotonous tasks, sometimes until dark, and at the end of their day, 'reading a book was probably the last thing that many workers wanted to do. And the light to enable them to make out the page was not available'.[53] The window tax was only repealed in 1851, which means that until that point the average home tended to be extremely dark, with candles and rush lights (which were expensive) used as the sometimes only source of light in working-class lodgings.[54] Such physical constraints meant that the reading of one individual number needed to be made appealing, exciting and to provide instant pleasure and gratification (though short-lived). These characteristics became the tools of serialisation as they bore more importance than the overall story arc or character developments: though episodes 'had to be attached, like cars in a train, to the past and the future', each one 'had to contain its own unity and interest'.[55] This goal, along with the conditions of production, is the reason why penny bloods were sometimes repetitive, with an inconsistent plot or flat characters. Such arguments often made by critics only reflect the fact that serial works were evaluated in comparison to literary works read as a single volume or even as three volumes, i.e. with inappropriate tools. To measure works that belong to the sphere of penny serialisation, other characteristics suited to a simply different aim must prevail. Indeed, repetitive plots and stereotypical characters actually helped build up the reader's interest and enjoyment, as they demonstrated the systemic nature of the social ills denounced in the penny blood.[56] The lack of teleology was thus not a failure on the part of the text, which did not aim towards the completion of one narrative arc from beginning to end, the way a novel would. On the contrary, the Victorian serial was built on a rhythm of 'progress and pause', as Linda K. Hughes and Michael Lund explain (1991), and the familiar generic structures secured the readership's attention thanks to their regularity and their repetitiveness. In other words, the appeal of the serial for the reader came from form as well, and not merely content, which aligns with the recurring theorisation of seriality as a 'game of repetition and variation'[57] or between 'repetition and innovation'.[58] Ruth Mayer even talks of the 'looped quality' of seriality, which emphasises both the circular quality inherent to seriality and its absence of a teleological end.[59] All in all, seriality studies scholars have consistently demonstrated over the past decades that seriality can also be 'understood as a narratological and poetological principle',[60] not merely as a mode of production and publication. This allows us to reframe the characteristics of the penny dreadful as fulfilling an important, productive function rather than betraying a supposed lack of quality, as contemporary critics decried.

The inherent fragmentation of the serial played a part in its pivotal role in the Victorian literary landscape, too. Hughes and Lund posit that the reading process itself made literature meaningful in a different way as the unavoidable pause in the narration enforced by the end of one instalment and the necessary wait until the next provided readers with time to reassess the narrated events and situation, perhaps in relation to their own world.[61] In the case of penny literature, the weekly rhythm of publication and the short length of instalments created a process that is specific to the genre, in that it was adapted to its readers' lives and the actual time they could dedicate to the work and to this assessment. The fact that a story had not yet reached an end made it more suited to such reflection, following Julia McCord Chavez's convincing argument on the Victorian serial as a form that fosters digression and 'with its enforced interruptions, embodies an equivalent model of wandering reading'.[62] Interestingly, Chavez builds her claim on John Ruskin's radical piece of art criticism in 'The Nature of Gothic' (1851–1853), in which he stressed the 'productive nature of wandering [...] in an age obsessed with order, control, and mechanical reproduction'[63] and argued for the superiority of the imperfect, rather than the perfect, asserting that 'the demand for perfection is always a sign of misunderstanding of the ends of art'.[64] Ruskin's view of perfection as an inherently limiting notion is in direct opposition with Matthew Arnold's belief that culture 'is, or ought to be, the study and pursuit of perfection'[65]; and seeing as serialised cheap fiction went against the grain of what was expected in terms of literature, Chavez's choice to rely on Ruskin's argument perfectly elucidates the tensions elicited by this shift in literary practices. The serial nature of cheap fiction such as penny bloods and their nonteleological structure thus 'emphasiz[e] the idea of reading as process, rather than text as product' – a process with a new rhythm that is less contemplative and more dynamic – and open up productive (and potentially subversive) spaces, which Chavez calls the 'Gothic heart of Victorian serial fiction'.[66] Serialised works such as penny fiction were a lively medium in constant evolution, which reflected daily experiences but also created space for reflection, and was made relatable by its very nature.

The experience provided by sensationalist serialised tales was therefore tied with an ephemeral quality that was at odds with and threatening to the idea of building towards improvement and stability advocated by the upper classes. They 'provided a common experience and [...] common memory'[67] for which the collective aspect mattered to be able to access the sense of community created around the reading of these tales. 'Sensations offer no greater pleasure than this', Diamond concludes[68]; crucially, the emphasis on enjoying the experience of these periodical sensations connects to the pivotal part played by the tales' sensationalism in forging a place for penny bloods in a new landscape of mass culture and literature.

Notes

1. Rose, 'How Historians Study', 209.
2. Willes, *Reading Matters*, 195.
3. Mayhew, *London Labour*, 1: 27–28.
4. Ibid., 1: 27.
5. Ibid.
6. Ibid., emphasis original.
7. Ibid., 3: 370.
8. Ibid.
9. Willes, *Reading Matters*, 194.
10. Ibid., 193.
11. Ibid.
12. Rose, 'Foreword', xii.
13. Ibid., xiii.
14. Willes, *Reading Matters*, 193.
15. Ibid.
16. Flanders, *The Invention of Murder*, 378.
17. Jacobs, 'Disvaluing the Popular', 95.
18. Ibid.
19. Ibid.
20. Foucault, *Discipline and Punish*, 180.
21. Deacon, 'Moral Orthopedics', 85.
22. Ibid., 91.
23. Foucault, *Discipline and Punish*, 219.
24. Ibid., 159.
25. Jacobs, 'Disvaluing the Popular', 96.
26. See Burz-Labrande 2021.
27. Cox, *Among the Doctors*, 17; see also Rose, 'Rereading the English Common Reader', 47–70.
28. Willes, *Reading Matters*, 194.
29. Bowley, *Wages*, 66.
30. Porter, *London: A Social History*, 176.
31. Carlisle, 'Popular and Mass-Market Fiction', 141.
32. Mayhew, *London Labour*, 2: 114.
33. Ibid., 1: 28.
34. Diamond, *Victorian Sensation*, 288.
35. Arnold, *Culture and Anarchy*, 53.
36. Mayhew, *London Labour*, 1: 27.
37. Ibid., 28.
38. Bolton, 'Cockney', 225.
39. See for instance Haywood 2002; Humpherys and James 2008; Basdeo 2019; Conary and Shannon 2023.
40. Bolton, 'Cockney', 223.
41. Trusler qtd. in Willes, *Reading Matters*, 195.
42. Wynne, *Sensation Novel*, 11.
43. Mieszkowski and Straumann, 'Force Fields', 154.
44. Hughes and Lund, *Victorian Serial*, 1.

45 See Hughes and Lund 1991; Law 2000; Delafield 2015.
46 Mieszkowski and Straumann, 'Force Fields', 151–152.
47 Voltaire qtd. in Colclough, *Consuming Texts*, viii.
48 Woodmansee, 'Genius', 429.
49 Garrett, *Gothic Reflections*, x.
50 Hughes and Lund, *Victorian Serial*, 7.
51 See Burz-Labrande 2021 and 2023.
52 Hughes and Lund, *Victorian Serial*, 8–9.
53 Willes, *Reading Matters*, 195.
54 Altick, *English Common Reader*, 92–93.
55 Bleiler, 'Introduction', 786.
56 See Humpherys, 'Introduction to G. W. M. Reynolds's "Encyclopedia of Tales"' in Humpherys and James, 123–132.
57 Kelleter, *Serial Narrative*, 3, 7–8.
58 Eco, 'Interpreting Serials', 96; see also Hutcheon, *Adaptation*, 8; Loock, 'Serial Narratives', 5.
59 Mayer, *Serial Fu Manchu*, 7.
60 Straumann, 'Viktorianische Roman', 164.
61 Hughes and Lund, *Victorian Serial*, 12.
62 Chavez, 'Gothic Heart', 792, 797.
63 Ibid., 792–793.
64 Ruskin, 'Nature of Gothic', 121.
65 Arnold, *Culture and Anarchy*, 53.
66 Chavez, 'Gothic Heart', 800, 792.
67 Diamond, *Victorian Sensation*, 288.
68 Ibid.

Chapter 2

SENSATIONALISM AND ENTERTAINMENT

A wholly different mode of circulation of literature among a new working-class audience modified the literary landscape in terms of content as well as format. Cheap publications in the first half of the nineteenth century move from a focus on improvement to mass entertainment: consumption takes precedence, and this new form of entertainment trumps the previously favoured long-term investment in activities linked to learning and bettering oneself. The new frenzy for serialisation of cheap fiction takes over, providing temporary pleasure through regular consumption rather than instruction, which required commitment to longer works.

One of the staples of penny blood and penny dreadful writing is their sensationalism: whether through violence, suspense, surprise or humour, the goal was to make an impression on the readership and prompt them to read further or buy another number. As an early group in penny dreadful categorisation, penny bloods are particularly interesting as these publications – ranging from the 1830s to the 1850s – precede the rise of the sensation novel, which reached a popularity peak in the 1860s. Indeed, the earliest uses of the term 'sensation' and 'sensationalism' recorded in the UK in a literary context occur in 1862, in the *Oxford Magazine* and the *Athenaeum* literary magazine.[1] The works traditionally considered as foundational of the sensation novel as a genre were published between 1859 and 1862: *The Woman in White* by Wilkie Collins; *East Lynne* by Mrs Henry Wood; and *Lady Audley's Secret* by Mary Elizabeth Braddon. Although Lyn Pykett has stressed the importance of looking beyond what Andrew Maunder calls 'this "A" list trio',[2] scholars agree that the three novels, and the decade of the 1860s more generally, retain a position considered central to the genre's development and popularity.[3] The penny bloods' publication dates therefore guarantee that neither their literary techniques nor their popularity can stem from the later sensation novels' success; rather, as Andrew King demonstrates, it is this 'literature of the kitchen' that helps understand the later sensation fiction 'of the drawing room' in many ways.[4]

As predecessors of sensation fiction, penny publications develop their own form of popular sensationalism, anchored not in artistic originality but in their very production circumstances as staples of entertainment culture and commodities in a fast-growing capitalistic market.

Entertainment and Literary Appropriation

Though they are less remembered now, penny blood imitations and plagiarisms of novels were very common in the late 1830s and the 1840s, demonstrating that middle-class literature was interesting to working-class readers, too, despite their not being the target audience. In this case, the phrase 'penny blood' is arguably problematic, as it only evokes the violent sensationalism found in a large number of early-Victorian popular works, effacing a variety of core entertainment features such as humour or romance in spite of their major place in the narratives.[5] But a wide range of stories published by the very same publishers and in the exact same format were so-called domestic romances and/or imitations of the most recent popular fiction. This incongruence can be explained by the fact that contemporary as well as later nineteenth-century criticism focused particularly on their supposedly immoral content to argue against penny publications and attempt to lower their popularity,[6] thus erasing their other characteristics for posterity. Research engaging with cheap periodical fiction of the 1840s must therefore reappropriate the phrase 'penny bloods' and expand it as a chronological categorisation of penny fiction, thereby including the important entertainment trend of humorous sensationalism that they encompassed instead of adopting a narrower scope restricted to publications which critics attempted to discredit as violent at the time.

Victorian popular culture was the age of literary piracy, from dramatizations on the London stage of yet unfinished serialised works to the circulation of unauthorised, pirated copies of British works in America. The market of literary appropriation constituted a major part of penny publications, which produced imitations at a strikingly fast pace. This was, of course, before the Literary Copyright Act was passed in the UK in 1842, guaranteeing that works be protected either for the duration of the life of the author plus an additional seven years, or for a total of forty-two years, depending on which was longer.[7] Before then, penny writers could thus revel in this potential market and appropriate best-sellers at will – and they certainly did, as Charles Dickens's fiction, for example, famously underwent this instant literary appropriation by Thomas Peckett Prest under the provocative pseudonym of 'Bos', an obvious pun on Dickens's own pseudonym 'Boz'. Peckett Prest was an extremely prolific writer for

Edward Lloyd of all styles of penny fiction including Dickens plagiarisms from 1837 and until the Copyright Act was passed. His works include the very popular *Post-Humurous (sic) Notes of the Pickwickian Club* (1837) – often referred to as *The Penny Pickwick* – *The Life and Adventures of Oliver Twiss, the workhouse boy* (1837), *The Sketch-Book* (1837), *David Copperful* (1838), *Nickelas Nickelbery* (1838), *Pickwick in America!* (1838–1839), *Mister Humfries' Clock* (1840) and *Barnaby Budge* (1841). Although Dickens's serialisation of *The Pickwick Papers* (1836–1837) already made fiction more affordable for middle-class and lower-class readers, the price of two shillings per monthly part remained too expensive for a large group of potential readers, and the numerous illegal spinoffs sold for a fraction of the price soon multiplied. Lloyd's *Penny Pickwick* series claimed sales of about 50,000 numbers a week, which is far superior to the numbers available through Dickens's publishers Chapman and Hall, recording about 40,000 monthly copies sold.[8] Of course, Lloyd's numbers, in this case, are claims found in weekly prefaces and thus function more as a commercial argument than as actual records. But the sheer number of plagiarisms circulating at the time and issued by various publishing houses does make it likely that more people read these than Dickens's originals. Some of Lloyd's imitations also benefited from the fact that the titles as well as front-page designs were intended to bear striking resemblances to Dickens's works. In a marketplace where popularity depended as much – if not more – on hearsay as on advertisement, potential customers could easily have heard of *Sketches by Boz* and, thus inspired, bought a number bearing a similar-sounding drop-head title (Figure 2.1).

Similarly, the design of *Nickelas Nickelbery*'s drop-head title resembles that of the frontispiece of *Nicholas Nickleby*, disclosing the same sort of information in a comparable order in the subtitle as well as using a very similar style of drawn title (see Figures 2.2 and 2.3). Although Dickens's work came with rich and ornate illustrations by Hablot Browne or George Cruikshank, in stark contrast with the simplicity of a Lloyd number, the familiarity of the names

THE
SKETCH-BOOK ᴏғ 'BOS

Figure 2.1 Drop-head title of instalment number 7 of *The Sketch-Book by 'Bos'*, i.e. Thomas Peckett Prest, published by Edward Lloyd (p. 49). By permission of the British Library.

THE LIFE AND ADVENTURES OF

CONTAINING

A FAITHFUL ACCOUNT OF THE

Fortunes, Misfortunes, Uprisings, Downfallings,

AND

COMPLETE CAREER OF THE NICKLEBY FAMILY.

 **EDITED BY " BOZ."**

Figure 2.2 Frontispiece of instalment number 11 of *Nicholas Nickleby*, written by Charles Dickens as 'Boz'. From: Charles Dickens, *The Life and Adventures of Nicholas Nickleby*, inserted between xvi and 1.

and designs certainly prompted sales as well, whether customers were aware that they were not buying the original work or not.

Nickelas Nickelbery was published in 1838, the same year as *Nicholas Nickleby*. This almost instantaneous publication of the Bos imitation of an original Dickens work was rather typical: only a few weeks or months lie between *The Pickwick Papers* (1836–1837) and *The Penny Pickwick* (1837), between *Sketches by Boz* (1837–1839) and *The Sketch-Book* (1837), between *Oliver Twist* and *Oliver*

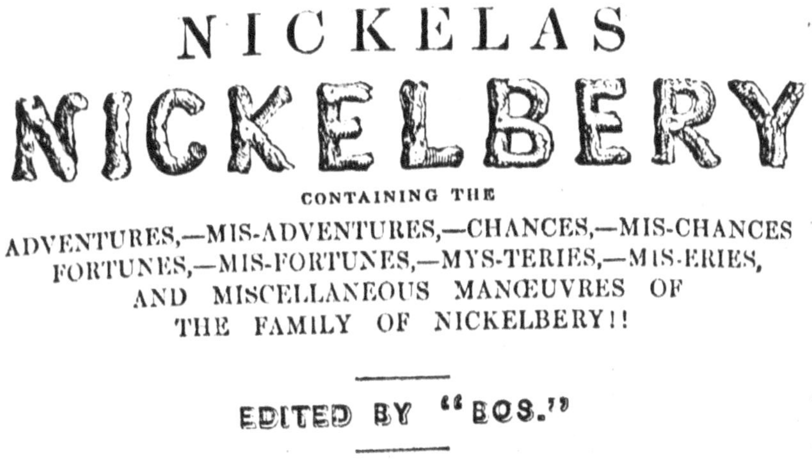

NICKELAS NICKELBERY

CONTAINING THE

ADVENTURES,—MIS-ADVENTURES,—CHANCES,—MIS-CHANCES
FORTUNES,—MIS-FORTUNES,—MYS-TERIES,—MIS-ERIES,
AND MISCELLANEOUS MANŒUVRES OF
THE FAMILY OF NICKELBERY!!

EDITED BY "BOS."

Figure 2.3 Drop-head title of instalment number 1 of *Nickelas Nickelbery*, written by Thomas Peckett Prest as 'Bos' and published by Edward Lloyd (p. 1). By permission of the British Library.

Twiss (both beginning in 1837), and the list goes on. *Nickelas Nickelbery* stands out in terms of simultaneity, as the first weekly number appeared on the very same day as the first monthly number of *Nicholas Nickleby*, which Adam Abraham points out as 'perhaps unprecedented in the annals of imitation'.[9] Consequently, the first weekly instalment attempts to imitate something that the author himself has not read yet, which results in 'pages [padded out] as best he could'[10] until he could read the monthly part and rely on it for the following weekly instalments. From then on, though, the text by Bos follows the original closely and paraphrases it repeatedly.[11] This publication is what prompted Dickens's famous 'Proclamation' published on 28 February 1838, in which he stated his abhorrence of the situation and of penny writers, or 'pirates',[12] who plagiarised his work.[13] This proclamation crystallised the tensions raised by literary piracy around the definition of authorial ownership, the importance of access to literature and the different legal frameworks with no international copyright agreement in place.[14] But it also provided penny publisher Lloyd with an opportunity to clarify his own place in the developing landscape of mass entertainment: a few weeks later, on 31 March 1838, Lloyd issued a humorously written *Nickelbery* 'proclamation' which directly answered and mocked Dickens's, with almost word for word parallels in places.[15] However, the more words accumulate, the more absurd the proclamation becomes, losing meaning as it progresses and suggesting that Dickens's public notice took itself too seriously. Tellingly, this tongue-in-cheek reaction was published in the penny magazine *Cleave's London Satirist and Gazette of Variety*, which underscores its satirical quality. Further, Louis James describes it as 'a very fair parody of Dickens's notice set up in identical type' which reveals that it parodies and imitates both content and form[16] – a technique reproduced in many other Bos imitations. With this dialogue between the publications, penny plagiarisms situate themselves within several levels of entertainment, as the plagiarism of an already popular author takes on a parodic quality while further circulating similar topoi. Though not directly sensational, literary appropriations and plagiarisms demonstrate that the penny blood format has its roots in entertainment, as the goal to entertain is at the heart of all variations of the penny blood, whether humorous or horrific, and is constantly furthered by the development of and experimentation with a variety of sensational features, which I will examine in the next sections.

The Penny Bloods' Own Form of Sensationalism

Sensationalism spontaneously evokes plot twists and suspense between chapters or numbers; but this is actually not how it mostly manifests in penny bloods. Rather than authorial intent and plot development, the conditions of production of penny publications governed how much content would be included in the issue and at which point the story would break off. To produce as much as possible for the minimum of costs, the double columns which traditionally constituted a page had to be filled to the very end. As is visible in Lloyd's as well as Reynolds's publications, leaving a blank space on the page was not an option, since it would have been economically inefficient. The allocated space would be filled according to the criterion of how much room was available on the page – even if it sometimes meant cutting a scene in half until the next instalment. The reader would find the action interrupted sometimes very abruptly, and the following weekly number would pick up where it left off without so much of a 'previously, in [...]'. However, leaving the readership hanging with a particular event had to be done in a way that ensured the safety of the economic model of the penny blood: to keep the interest of the readership, other ways of inducing suspense and getting the reader hooked had to be found.

To engage and retain its readership, the penny blood had to make the most of the available medium while finding a way around its material restrictions, and circulation numbers seem to indicate that they succeeded in doing so. It should be noted that in most penny publications of the time, illustrations were rather rare, as they cost too much money to justify a high number in each instalment. Lloyd's *People's Periodical and Family Library*, for example, featured between one and two illustrations per instalment in 1846–1847, at the time of one of its most famous publications *The String of Pearls: A Romance*.[17] The cover would include an illustration related to the issue's main story (which alternated every other week with another featured story), and a second illustration could sometimes be found along with an instalment of yet another story around the issue's middle. The front page illustration was usually concerned with 'provoking public interest or excitement', that is, the primary meaning of sensationalism[18]: from an obviously distressed female character sobbing in her chair (Figure 2.4) to a suspenseful illustration of the barber reaching for a threatening razor when faced with officers and a dog (Figure 2.5), the front pages of *The String of Pearls* clearly aimed to make the reader curious.

Sensationalism did not only equal shock or suspense, but romance too, signalled in the subtitle of the work and illustrated on the front page of issue 11 (Figure 2.6). This portrait of Johanna Oakley and Mark Ingestrie is not a reference to any precise scene as the two hardly have any time together during the narrative, until they reunite in the final chapter. But it clearly relies on an imagery of love, resembling a medallion and framed with floral ornaments and doves, with a heart hanging above the two lovers. The inclusion of one constant illustration on the front page of the issue

Figure 2.4 Front page illustration of issue 7 of Edward Lloyd's *The People's Periodical and Family Library* (p. 97). By permission of the British Library.

Figure 2.5 Front page illustration of issue 8 of Edward Lloyd's *The People's Periodical and Family Library* (p. 113). By permission of the British Library.

was therefore clearly intended as a marketing tool, appealing to potential customers and prompting them to buy. While one could refer back to the illustration when reading a related scene, it bore more of an advertising quality and could only have a limited impact in terms of the reading experience given that it never came simultaneously with the event it depicted, but always before the reading had even started, pre-structuring reader expectations. If these penny blood illustrations did attach some form of sensationalism to their stories, they were therefore clearly not enough to sustain it throughout the story and between numbers. Other techniques had to produce this desired effect.

With so little leeway in terms of layout, breaks or visual components, the written text was the only element that could be used to play around with the penny bloods' own form of sensationalism. In this context, the narrative situation is a particularly relevant contributing factor in the creation of sensationalist storytelling. A very present heterodiegetic omniscient narrator often participates in shrouding the story in mystery by providing hints, directly addressing readers and stepping out of the story only to instantly deny them more information. Phrasings such as 'but we must not anticipate' or 'we may pass over [this conversation]' are extremely frequent and stress

PORTRAITS OF JOHANNA OAKLEY AND MARK INGESTRIE.

Figure 2.6 Front page illustration of issue 11 of Edward Lloyd's *The People's Periodical and Family Library* (p. 161). By permission of the British Library.

the orchestrated nature of the narration; and the narrator often pretends to be on the side of the reader, using a knowing 'we' to create collusion with the reader, e.g. 'as we dislike useless mysteries, we may as well explain that [...]' or 'we must not however allow the reader to remain in the same state of mystification'.[19] The frequent metalepses putting the story on hold while the narrator intervenes however soon reveal that the narrator is unreliable and masterminds the whole narrative, manipulating the readers and creating said 'useless mysteries'. Claiming 'we must not anticipate'[20] is rather ironical when the narrator is in fact the one who chooses to do so, playing with information and distilling it expertly to maintain tension. The narrator equally stresses their role in ensuring the fluidity of the narration: for instance, declaring 'we may pass over [...] skipping a conversation [...] we will presume that they have breakfasted, and that they are at the shop of a clothier' gives the impression of a fast-forward to avoid any form of stasis in storytelling.[21] These metanarrative remarks spell out a decision-making process which reminds readers that the narrator is not only omniscient indeed, but all-powerful, and merely deciding not to share some of the details. Readers are only given the information that the narrator chooses to disclose; and following the narrating gaze on events comes with a certain visual quality, too. Such comments as 'while she is courting repose, [...] we will take a glance at the parlour below'[22] bring to the modern reader's mind a crane shot, where the camera would move to a different level of the house. Within this parallel, the penny blood narrator thus acts as both voice-over and director, giving the impression of curated storytelling specifically tailored to sensationalism.

In the case of particular penny bloods, such as *The String of Pearls*, the narrator ensures the advancement of the different storylines by orchestrating a certain movement between various narrative levels. The different plotlines progress at a separate pace and are seemingly managed by the narrator who leads readers mostly to and fro from Tobias's (Sweeney Todd's apprentice) to Johanna's perspective, but also through different embedded narratives. All of them present sensationalist interjections mingling with inner focalization – one example of this is Colonel Jeffery's very lively travel narrative, filled with exclamations such as 'Alas!' or adjectives such as 'fearful and agonizing'.[23] Overall, the narration seems to expand synchronically, made of several threads unravelling from one temporal spot. The different embedded voices have different functions and narrative weights. Some of the voices help move the plot forward by giving out pieces of answers every time (such as the Colonel, who on a metadiegetic level acts as a storyteller himself by revealing a little more each time he speaks to Johanna); others do not per se but fulfil other functions. This is the case of the 'Mad Woman's Tale' in Chapter 30: the character is enclosed in space, as she is in a lunatic asylum, just like her narrative is enclosed in the story, and this embedded narrative adds to the Gothic atmosphere while importantly giving a voice to a socially marginalized, rejected figure. In this case, the various embedded narratives become a form of polyvocal narration, as voices of different social status are given the power to contribute to the narrative. While such embedded narratives are not a staple of all penny bloods, when used, they actively contribute to a sensationalized form of storytelling as the development of the narration travels from one person to the next under the aegis of the omniscient narrator.

On a level closer to form than to narrative content, chapter breaks themselves participate in creating and sustaining sensationalism throughout the publications, too, through a very particular mode of functioning. As previously explained, an instalment would often end abruptly at the end of a page or of the space allocated to a story. In some recent penny blood re-editions, such as Robert L. Mack's edition of *The String of Pearls: A Romance*,[24] the original segmentation for publication is visually indicated on the page (e.g. with a short centred rule between two paragraphs or with a centred horizontal line of asterisks) to allow modern readers to see where the weekly part would have stopped at the original time of publication. This allows twenty-first-century audiences to realise that for Victorian readers, more often than not, chapters were actually interrupted from one week to the next rather than coming to an end within one single instalment. Although penny publications do include chapters, i.e. a traditional construction belonging to literary narration, they hijack their original purpose as the story is paused somewhere else due to material constraints. The break induced by a chapter change takes on another dimension and comes to signal a change of scene, of geographical location, of character focus. But it is rarely used for real narrative suspense, as readers would almost always have had access to the beginning of the next chapter. The potential (but fake) suspense that comes with the end of a chapter, therefore, fulfils the function of a sensationalist tool that provides added thrill to the reader and enhances desire to keep reading; but interestingly, it also satisfies this desire instantly, going against class-related debates about the moral value of delayed gratification. In the case of a chapter break, the action is only delayed symbolically by the small blank on the page, but readers would almost instantly find out whether the actual fulfilment lived up to what was imagined. In his theorisation of cliffhangers, Luke Terlaak Poot stresses that not every sensational turn in the story is a cliffhanger, as the cliffhanger requires the urgency of an interrupted scene; but his discussion of the 'continuous cliffhanger'[25] is relevant in the case of penny blood chapter breaks in which the action continues straight away in the next chapter. That the interrupted action is quickly resolved does not matter in itself: through this extra-diegetic pause, the cliffhanger 'imbues its chosen moment with significance by rendering it an open question for the reader',[26] and sensationalism aims at creating exactly such a thrill or emotional response in the first place. Chapter sequencing in penny bloods participates in this goal.

In addition to their potential for narrative tension, chapter breaks also were used to cater to readers' potential preferences on the level of the story: two chapters following one another in the same instalment could focus on different main characters, locations or subplots. One instalment could thus have more variety than if it had contained a single but complete chapter and please a broader audience as it intermingled different sorts of plots – that way, a single instalment had better odds at satisfying, for instance, both the reader who wants romance and the reader looking for a gloomy storyline.

In so doing, penny bloods paradoxically foreshadow what has been called 'narrative complexity' in recent scholarship concerned with television studies, in that they 'oscillate between long-term arc storytelling and stand-alone episodes'.[27] This effort to ensure variety could however lead to plotlines multiplying and potentially disappearing, as the episodic nature of serial fiction 'encourage[d] the throwing forward of narrative lines' even if they might not all end up developed.[28] Such potential incoherencies were criticised as proof of the penny bloods' supposed bad quality. As the self-designated London Hermit humorously described in 1875, suspense could be artificially added in the story for the mere reason that the physical number or page was at its end, even if this produced plot inconsistencies in the middle of a chapter:

> Bottom of last page of number, where story breaks off [...] *must* be something startling, so as to lead them on to take next number [*sic*], even if you have to cut a chapter out of the middle to make it fit in. It never matters what plot you take, or whether you have any at all, so long as the incidents are sensational [...].[29]

The seriality component of penny bloods was not so much a literary choice than a need arising through their publication and circulation circumstances, but writers attempted to appropriate this seriality in order to maximise commercial success and play with expectations: something startling at the end of the number could create mystery to hook the readers, even if it turned out to have very little significance in the story. The takeaway here is that as non-teleological narratives, penny bloods functioned within a different set of rules – their seriality meant that the emphasis was on producing an entertaining number. Sensationalism helped penny fiction achieve just that, and the quality of the entertainment provided was what would make a serial popular, rather than the complexity or consistency of its plot. Beyond the simplistic criticism of their quality, such ends of instalments encapsulate the penny bloods' entanglement of sensationalism and seriality to produce entertainment.

Experiments in Multimodal Sensationalism

Despite the restrictions of the written page in the cycle of cheap periodical production, and perhaps surprisingly, penny blood publications also present multimodal aspects, although they are 200-year-old static artefacts. As Eve Bearne points out, paper alone is a medium that can bear multimodal qualities even without being combined with literal sounds or illustrations, as 'different types of text have their own patterns of cohesion that contribute to the overall architecture of the text'.³⁰ The written text can thus use visual markers intended to accompany readers through their reading experience and help expand it, as the message 'is "spread across" different modes', which all contribute to its meaning.³¹ Though the cheap production of penny bloods did not allow for the use of different fonts, blank spaces or layout eccentricities, I argue that these mass-produced cheap publications purposely combine the short form with different modes within the verbal text 'communicated through paper',³² in order to maximise their potential for sensationalism.

In addition to chapter breaks, which already contribute to the development of a form of multimodal sensationalism through their visual presence on the page, another instance of a crucial visual feature of the penny bloods' sensationalism is the recurring use of typographical emphasis through italics, which either signal a specific event or give a specific narrative clue. In the same way that chapter breaks are indicated in recent reprints, italics have been consistently reproduced, which testifies to their relevance for the text. For example, in *The String of Pearls*, the revelation of Todd's murders having led to cannibalism is italicized in several instances, such as in the narration of the penultimate chapter:

> Hence was it that in one moment, as if by magic, Sweeney Todd's visitors disappeared, and there was the empty chair. No doubt, he trusted to a fall of about twenty feet below, on to a stone floor, to be the death of them, or, at all events, to stun them until he could go down to finish the murder, and – *to cut them up for Mrs Lovett's pies!* after robbing them of all money and valuables they might have about them.³³

This device returns in the very last chapter, as Mark Ingestrie announces the truth: 'Ladies and Gentlemen – I fear that what I am going to say will spoil your appetites; but the truth is beautiful at all times, and I have to state that Mrs Lovett's pies are made of *human flesh!*'³⁴ The choice of italics in these instances is a deliberate way of signalling a specific situation – here, the horror of the cannibalistic aspect of the murders – and of either triggering the appropriate emotion in the readers or reinforcing it. It can therefore be considered a multimodal contribution to the sensationalist quality that is so characteristic of penny bloods and dreadfuls.

In addition to visual hints on the page, the written text also presents another interesting dimension that can almost be considered as sound effects and as an echo of the oral storytelling tradition. In *The Adventures of Valentine Vaux; or, The Tricks of a Ventriloquist* (published by Lloyd and written by Peckett Prest as Timothy Portwine in 1840), the eponymous protagonist has a talent for imitating people's voices. His specialty is what was known as distant-voice ventriloquy, a model of ventriloquism which was popular in the early nineteenth century and consisted in creating 'acoustic illusions of distance and tone, replicating a variety of voices from characters in different places'.[35] The text signals to the reader whose voice is imitated through the transcription of different accents and sounds in the written text, as I will show presently. In what Christopher Pittard calls an 'act of textual ventriloquism',[36] this penny blood is itself an imitation of Henry Cockton's *Life and Adventures of Valentine Vox the Ventriloquist*, which was published in instalments in 1839–1840 but was more expensive, as one number would cost a shilling. As a result, Cockton's original text targeted a substantially different audience. Both the original and the penny blood plagiarism appear within (and inscribe themselves into) a particular cultural moment: the early Victorian period was marked by a 'peculiar fascination with voice and its spectral or acousmatic phenomena',[37] as practices such as shorthand and phonography revealed a concern with representing voice in writing.[38] In essence, while silent reading (i.e. with no audible phonetic sound) still implies inner articulation or 'endophony', as Garrett Stewart has argued in his theorization of the phonotext, Victorian reading practices as 'embodied vocal performance and mimicry at a number of levels, from public readings to the "performance" of the text among groups of friends or family'[39] make explicit Stewart's locating of 'embodied voice' as the *destination* of textuality.[40] Consequently, the concern with recording voice (and not simply speech) in writing leads to multimodal experimentations with the representation of accents and sounds.

In both *Valentine Vox* and *Valentine Vaux*, there are many instances of dialogues in which graphemes are rearranged to visually match the phonemes that will evoke the desired accent and create the right impact on the reader. However, although the storyline remains effectively the same in the two versions, the use of multimodality regarding sounds reveals drastically different intentions. In the original, working-class characters, such as Tooler the coach driver, are shown as having a very strong accent and dialect, and their speech is contrasted with that of another character, the 'gentleman in black':

> 'Well, blarm me!' cried Tooler. 'But, darng it all, he must be somewhere!'
> 'I'll taake my solemn davy,' said Bill, 'that he *was* there.'
> 'I seed um myself,' exclaimed Bob, 'wi my oarn oyes, an' didnt loike the looks on um a bit.'
> 'There cannot,' said the gentleman in black, 'be the smallest possible doubt about his having been there; but the question for our mature consideration is, where is he now?'[41]

The working-class is distinguished from the middle-class by its own specific code, which is visual on the page but also rings in readers' 'inner ear of silent reading'[42] as the accent comes to life so vividly that one cannot help but imagine it and hear it while reading. This experience and the aurality of the working-class code at stake here would have only been rendered more striking when reading the text out loud. Cockton's text illustrates the fact that coding speech as dialect often performs the function of identifying characters with a particular social class or region, and most importantly marking the characters' identity by distinguishing them from those around.[43] Additionally, this particular play on language shows social semiotics at work, as a concern with sentence grammar is combined with the phonemic characteristics of the accent that the text attempts to reproduce. Indeed, as the linguist and semiotician Michael Halliday explains, sentence grammar encapsulates the ways in which any language community expects a sentence to be patterned for it to make sense to that community.[44] But the term 'expectation' is key: as we go deeper in the working-class world with the penny blood plagiarism and its most likely poorer readership, the visual signs of accents shift. Unlike in *Valentine Vox*, the coach driver himself does not have distinctive speech anymore, but the contrast comes from the boy described as a 'yokel':

'Now, Bill,' said the coachman as soon as he had brought his unwieldy body to the ground, 'we've got something to do as will require an uncommon deal of care; so in the first place just run into the house and bring out your master's gun.'
'Why, what d'ye want a gnn for?' asked the yokel.[45]

In this example, the accent-feature relies not only on the reading experience but also on the expected readership. Given that the text presents a supposedly different readership from Cockton's, a different type of group distinction is introduced which reveals social hierarchies within the lower class itself, instead of marking the difference between middle- and lower-class as in the original text. Therefore, the coach driver speaks more clearly than the 'yokel', a usually derogatory term designating an uneducated and unsophisticated person from the countryside.[46] This feature supposes that readers themselves identify the difference (as in this case, the reader might have had an accent similar to the one that is phonetically transcribed onto the page). In the same way as with italics, these features rely on the written page's reception and on the experience of reading. Such passages would certainly invite performance when read out loud – reading aloud, after all, 'gives the page a voice that is and isn't the writer's, is and isn't the reader's'[47] – and would consequently provoke a change in tone or in voice, to do justice to the change in the typescript.

This reveals that purposeful multimodality is at work, here, in encoding a specific situation with a different mode in the verbal text.

The shift in social hierarchy revealed by the penny blood's use of multimodality aligns with the functioning of other penny plagiarisms of the late 1830s. As scholars of popular literature have demonstrated, the close similarities between penny plagiarisms and their original versions allow the former to utilise the original style and content and rework them to put pressure on literary representation.[48] James extensively compares *Oliver Twist* and *Oliver Twiss* and concludes that the latter's mode of writing is adapted to 'those with little training in reading and tastes shaped by contemporary popular theatre and broadsheets' thanks to heightened melodrama, more farce and cruder violence.[49] But he also finds more realism and more factual detail in city descriptions for instance, concluding that the penny adaptation addresses the surroundings and potential daily life of lower classes more directly than Dickens did,[50] similarly to what happens from *Valentine Vox* to *Valentine Vaux*. Penny plagiarisms did not merely reproduce the text, but presented a different angle on the imitated stories, since the target audience did not need the potential focus on raising awareness of their own social reality for the middle classes. Kristen Starkowski investigates this perspective further and argues that the popular penny press defines working-class modes of 'characterological novelty': by mapping and comparing the amount of narrative attention dedicated to minor characters in Dickens's *Oliver Twist* and Prest's *Oliver Twiss*, Starkowski convincingly claims that the penny version shifts the focus and brings minor characters to the foreground, challenging the traditional distinction between flat and round characters.[51] This would mean that the repetition and plagiarism of pre-existing middle-class literature was not only tailored to a new readership, but actually allowed for a productive space to rethink character position and challenge the current state of literary representation of the time. This in part joins the argument made by Jacobs, who following Hoggart's[52] and James's works claims that these texts 'engaged in a political struggle over the social meaning of literary representations, and thus confronted mainstream literature with the cultural fact of "heteroglossia"'.[53] Through the use of Mikhail Bakhtin's concept, Jacobs stresses the fact that these plagiarisms are in fact a reappropriation of literature by its new readership and that they are both a symptom of and a tool in the political struggle for visibility of the lower classes. *Valentine Vaux* showcases this concern in its multimodal focus on voices, social semiotics and speech coding that differ from Cockton's original. This appropriation of middle-class literature helped by multimodality allows for an expansion of its views and of its literary representations, simultaneously deconstructing it as well as enriching it with new potential.

Though the tone of this last example differs greatly from the more Gothic publications that gave penny bloods their moniker, such playful attempts at multimodality and appropriations are consistent with the other features of sensationalism noted in this chapter as they firmly anchor the penny blood in the realm of entertainment, therefore drawing on sensation in the primary sense of the term, with a goal to cause widespread interest. These various experimentations with the written page and its affordances all bear in common the fact that they reveal a certain creativity to meet the strict demands of a fast-paced and rapidly evolving market. Whether it is through their use of narrative voices, characters on the page, illustrations, suspense, chapter breaks, multimodality or re-circulation of middle-class literature as cheap literature, it becomes clear that penny bloods drew from their difficult production circumstances ingeniously to create their own forms of sensationalism and entertainment and successfully establish a readership, as well as borrow from the burgeoning contemporary mass culture in order to push their boundaries and develop a new genre of writing.

Notes

1 Oxford English Dictionary, s.v. 'sensationalism' and 'sensation', accessed 27 March 2025, http://www.oed.com/view/Entry/175942; http://www.oed.com/view/Entry/175940.
2 Maunder, 'Mapping', 19 qtd. in Pykett, *Sensation Novel*, 4.
3 See Tillotson, 'Lighter Reading', xvi; Edwards, *Mid-Victorian Thrillers*, 4; Loesberg, 'Ideology of Narrative Form', 115; Pykett, *Sensation Novel*, 4.
4 King, 'Literature of the Kitchen', 38.
5 Scholarship on penny bloods has recently turned to the wider range of stories and to questions of genre. For more on humour in penny bloods, see Frohn 2023.
6 See Burz-Labrande 2021 and 2023.
7 The 1814 Copyright Act had established a protection for twenty-eight years from the time of publication, but if the author was still alive by the end of this period, the protection would be extended 'for the residue of his natural life'. The bill was the object of great debates and was amended and re-committed several times. The absence of a definition of copyright allowed many plagiarisms to be published, though unauthorized.
8 Kaplan, *Dickens: A Biography*, ch. 3.
9 Abraham, 'Pseudo-Dickens Industry', 758.
10 Slater, *Composition and Monthly Publication of Nicholas Nickleby*, 19.
11 Abraham, 'Pseudo-Dickens Industry', 759; James, *Fiction for the Working Man*, 64.
12 Monica F. Cohen's *Pirating Fictions: Ownership and Creativity in Nineteenth-Century Popular Culture* (2017) provides a valuable study of the connections between maritime piracy and literary piracy in Victorian popular culture, in which she argues that 'the pirate becomes a vehicle of profound tension between an emergent ideal of intellectual property and a literary culture whose emphatically collective, derivative, citational character tends to confound claims of individual originality and ownership' (pp. 2–3).
13 Dickens, *Nicholas Nickleby*, 780.

14 Cohen, *Pirating Fictions*, 1–2.
15 *Cleave's London Satirist*, 'Nickelas Nickelbery', 4.
16 James, *Fiction for the Working Man*, 63.
17 *The String of Pearls* has been the topic of heated scholarly debates in relation to its authorship, seeing as it was published anonymously and no record from Lloyd's publishing house identifies its author with certainty. While James Malcolm Rymer is now recognised as its author (see Smith 2002, Collins 2010), I prefer to refer to it as *The String of Pearls* to preserve the focus on the texts itself as published, i.e. anonymously, leaving the author out to place the text centre stage.
18 Oxford English Dictionary, s.v. 'sensationalism', accessed 27 March 2025, http://www.oed.com/view/Entry/175942.
19 'The String of Pearls', 199, 86, 41, 276.
20 Ibid., 199.
21 Ibid., 86.
22 Ibid., 103.
23 Ibid., 83.
24 Published in 2007 under the title of *Sweeney Todd: The Demon Barber of Fleet Street*.
25 Terlaak Poot, 'On Cliffhangers', 64.
26 Ibid., 60.
27 Mittell, 'Narrative Complexity', 33.
28 Lansdown, 'Pickwick Papers', 78.
29 The London Hermit, 'Physiology of Penny Awfuls', 367, emphasis original.
30 Bearne, 'Multimodality', 158–159.
31 Kress, *Literacy in the New Media Age*, 35.
32 Bearne, 'Multimodality', 158.
33 'The String of Pearls', 277.
34 Ibid., 280.
35 Pittard, 'V for Ventriloquism', 4.
36 Ibid., 1.
37 Ibid., 1.
38 See Pitman 1845.
39 Pittard, 'V for Ventriloquism', 21.
40 Stewart, *Reading Voices*, 7, 3.
41 Cockton, *Valentine Vox*, 28.
42 Stewart, *Reading Voices*, 9.
43 Page, *Speech in the English Novel*, 55; see also Chapman 1994.
44 See Halliday 1978.
45 Portwine, *Valentine Vaux*, 19.
46 Oxford English Dictionary, s.v. 'yokel', accessed 27 March 2025, http://www.oed.com/view/Entry/232060.
47 Goldblatt, *Art and Ventriloquism*, 104.
48 See James 1981; Hoggart 1987; Cohen 2017; Starkowski 2019; Cohen 2021.
49 James, 'The View from Brick Lane', 94.
50 Ibid., 89.
51 Starkowski, 'Characterological Novelty', 290.
52 Hoggart, 'Travesties of Dickens', 32–36.
53 Jacobs, 'Disvaluing the Popular', 98.

Chapter 3

THE MAZE OF METROPOLITAN LIFE: URBANISING THE GOTHIC

The penny bloods' development of their own form of sensationalism and entertainment has its roots in various storytelling traditions, all belonging to some extent to the sphere of the popular. Louis James stresses that penny publications 'were written with considerable literary aspirations, and the fact that [many] were published and ran their full course indicates similar interests in many readers':[1] adapting the oral storytelling tradition into a cheap, short, serialised format that experimented with various literary techniques certainly proved successful among the new readers. In addition to borrowing from the newly developing mass culture of entertainment, penny bloods also reworked an older literary tradition to which their very name alludes and which contributes to the entertaining quality of their sensationalism: Among the 'glimmerings of past English literature' that they contain,[2] the penny bloods or early penny dreadfuls' most present influence is certainly the Gothic tradition and its thrills.

The Penny Bloods' Eighteenth-Century Gothic Legacy

The Gothic is most often defined as primarily a literature of excess, transgression and ambivalence. A 'highly unstable genre [that] scatter[s] its ingredients into various modes',[3] it traces, exposes and challenges contemporary or past norms and institutions, and its potential to destabilise can easily be transferred into new literary productions or genres thanks to a universally adaptable ability to 'engag[e] with the alienation from the past as both a repository of the fears of disintegration and the hopes of regaining a sense of unity and value', as Fred Botting phrases it.[4] From the eighteenth-century Gothic novel and chapbooks, it therefore continues to help engage with later times of upheaval and transition such as the fin-de-siècle, with what is now often referred to as late-Victorian Gothic, but also the early nineteenth century, in the case of penny bloods.

At a time when societal changes concerned just about every area of life, from the country's industrialisation to the literacy boom that created the working-class readership that is of primary concern here, it is no surprise that eighteenth-century Gothic (usually understood as Gothic fiction published between 1764 and roughly 1820) and its popular appeal would pass on a strong legacy to the literature of the following decades. Judith Flanders goes so far as to state that 'bloods developed out of late-eighteenth-century gothic tales',[5] with a similar format (often serialised tales, sold in wrappers and for cheap prices) and content. To back this up, she refers to George Augustus Sala, a prolific author and journalist who started his own career by illustrating and writing penny bloods, among other things. In 1862, he described these publications as

> a world of dormant peerages, of murderous baronets, and ladies of title addicted to the study of toxicology, of gipsies and brigand-chiefs, men with masks and women with daggers, of stolen children, withered hags, heartless gamesters, nefarious roués, foreign princesses, Jesuit fathers, gravediggers, resurrection-men, lunatics and ghosts.[6]

This wonderfully evocative description certainly highlights the strong classical Gothic legacy of penny bloods, which is also echoed in numerous titles such as *Angelina; or, the Mystery of St. Mark's Abbey* (1841), *Vileroy; or, the Horrors of Zindorf Castle* (1844), and of course, *Varney the Vampyre; or, the Feast of Blood* (1847). It must be noted that the word 'Gothic' was originally neither used to refer to eighteenth-century works nor to penny bloods, the term 'romances' being the universally preferred choice.[7] The way penny bloods presented themselves echoes this tendency: *Varney the Vampyre* as well as *The String of Pearls* both bear the subtitle 'A Romance', and many others were introduced as so-called domestic romances. From the first page, penny bloods therefore located themselves within close proximity to classical Gothic works.

Although publishers of late-eighteenth-century Gothic tales were struggling considerably by the beginning of the 1830s, the nineteenth century saw the Gothic tradition not only remain relevant, but evolve, too, as publications such as penny bloods appropriated it. The multiplying number of publications on the market and the development of printing presses, leading to a drop in prices, engendered a major shift in the marketplace which effectively pushed the popular Gothic chapbooks and pamphlets into decline. Charles Maturin, for instance, stated in 1816 that 'the tale of terror [...] was already "out" in 1807'.[8] However, this does not mean that the Gothic was disappearing; rather, as Robert Miles explains, it entered a new phase, an 'afterlife', particularly after 1820 when it began to 'migrat[e] into other forms and media'.[9] This new creative phase allowed the Gothic to reassert its legitimacy across the nineteenth century through 'flamboyant plays and scattered operas, short stories and fantastic tales for magazines and newspapers, "sensation" novels for women and the literate working-class [...] and substantial resurgences of full-fledged Gothic novels'[10] – among which were penny bloods and penny dreadfuls. Gothic propensities for the sensational aligned conveniently with the penny format, as they aimed to ensure 'the reader feels a quiver of fear' without necessarily requiring character or plot build-up.[11] This explains in part why penny bloods were able to find their way into the 1840s and blended historical and domestic romances with romantic poetry imagery, allegorical representations and Gothic thrills.[12] While penny bloods should not be considered Gothic romances in the sense of the tale of terror established by authors such as Ann Radcliffe and Matthew G. Lewis, it is appropriate to talk of Gothic legacy, of literary influence.

The 'mix-and-match' approach of penny bloods in circulating among popular genres and appropriating certain elements is key to understanding their nature and function.[13] Though penny bloods are undoubtedly marked by a strong Gothic legacy, they also 'rehandle' the Gothic type,[14] actively mixing it with other popular traditions. E. F. Bleiler formulates this technique rather clearly, arguing that

> it is an error to consider the penny dreadful as simply a Gothic continuation. It borrowed the subject matter of crime from the factual criminal chapbooks and the Newgate novel, from which it also took a peculiar episodic structure. And from the more formal novel of the period, Ainsworth, Marryat, Cooper, Bulwer and Dickens, it picked whatever it found useful. The common factor was thrill or sensation.[15]

Driven by a desire to assess the readers' tastes and push boundaries rather than inscribe themselves within a specific, existing genre, penny bloods can be described as a fluid, dynamic literary form. Interacting with the various popular trends, they retained a form of freedom which allowed them to keep adapting and evolving, liberating themselves from the anxiety of influence theorised by Harold Bloom in 1973, that is to say, from the detrimental impact of literary influence which Bloom argued takes shape in an oedipal struggle raised by the potential weight of literary predecessors. This also explains the wide range of penny fiction across the century, as well as middle- and upper-class criticism of their literary quality, since they did not fit in any existing category or follow established literary rules. As James formulates it, penny-blood writing is the result of 'several traditions of literature [...] mixed by literary hacks eager for material, and suspended in a jargon of melodrama'.[16] In the 1840s, penny blood publications therefore toyed with several threads of literary tendencies – among which eighteenth-century Gothic – to assess their readership's tastes, interweaving them in their own tapestry.

The penny bloods' appropriation of the Gothic tradition of storytelling makes particular sense when considering their position in society and in the marketplace. 'From its beginnings', Peter K. Garrett tells us, 'Gothic fiction has taken an oppositional stance' which involved 'resistance to the constraints of the ordinary, the norms'.[17] Given the penny publications' place as outsiders in the literary marketplace and their rejection from the higher spheres, their very format along with a content labelled as too dark or immoral encapsulate a resistance to the expectations of the higher classes and an opposition to the norms of literary publication at the time. This resistance might not always have been a conscious decision by publishers or writers, but even this uncertainty echoes Gothic fiction, which Garrett states is sometimes 'credited with deliberate subversion; sometimes it is read symptomatically for the ways its terrors betray cultural anxieties [...] about whatever threatens the dominant social order or challenges its ideologies'.[18] Just like Gothic fiction, thus, penny bloods embody a form of resistance to the hegemony, some of them (but not all) deliberately subversive, like Reynolds's *Mysteries of London* and its openly political critique of a corrupted aristocracy.[19] Simultaneously they can be read as a symptom of current cultural anxieties, with such texts as *The String of Pearls* and its description of the metropolis as threatening. This also explains the similar treatment that Gothic literature and the penny blood received by their contemporary critics: 'art Gothic' was favoured to so-called 'trade Gothic', which was quickly dismissed as 'literary rubbish' despite constituting a vast proportion of the most popular publications, as demonstrated by Franz J. Potter.[20] However, if 'art Gothic' had indeed come to a halt by the 1830s–1840s, 'trade Gothic' and the larger phenomenon of the Gothic in the literary marketplace were very much alive in and through publications such as penny bloods.

The influence of the tale of terror on penny bloods can be traced through various themes: the victory of good over evil, heightened moral issues, a potentially Faustian story, a castle- or prison-like setting allowing for unified stage properties.[21] *Varney the Vampyre*, for example, clearly exploits its Gothic roots as the story opens with what seems an almost perfect display of eighteenth-century Gothic characteristics: on a dark and stormy night, with a female protagonist reading alone by a dim light in an old house full of strange noises. Atmospheric descriptions continue to rely on this Gothic potential throughout the story: 'The solemn tones of an old cathedral clock have announced midnight – the air is thick and heavy – a strange, death like stillness pervades all nature'.[22] Virtually every chapter title contains words belonging to the lexical fields of either mystery, suddenness, danger, night or vampirism, and in many ways, the treatment of its vampire protagonist echoes John Polidori's *The Vampyre* (1819), often considered as the 'prototype of the literary vampire'.[23] One of the issues that James raises about considering the Gothic as living through penny bloods such as *Varney the Vampyre* is that 'conscious of the scepticism of his urban readers, Rymer arranges that it can all be explained'.[24] But this tension can be resolved thanks to the distinction established in the eighteenth century by Ann Radcliffe between 'terror Gothic' and 'horror Gothic', which Jerrold E. Hogle explains as part of a continuum:

> the first of these holds characters and readers mostly in anxious suspense about threats to life, safety, and sanity kept largely out of sight or in shadows or suggestions from a hidden past, while the latter confronts the principal characters with the gross violence of physical or psychological dissolution, explicitly shattering the assumed norms (including the repressions) of everyday life with wildly shocking, and even revolting, consequences.[25]

The example of *Varney the Vampyre* where 'it can all be explained' can indeed be identified as outside of 'terror Gothic', but the less mysterious, unabashed horror certainly places it – and other penny bloods, such as the cannibalistic, human-flesh-in-pies story of *The String of Pearls* – under the umbrella of 'horror Gothic', confronting its characters and readers with a destabilisation of everyday life norms. Penny bloods, therefore, not only bear the legacy of eighteenth-century Gothic, but participate in the evolution of the Gothic phenomenon in literature. By appropriating the genre and recycling it into their own form of sensationalism as a direct consequence of their social and cultural context, penny bloods pioneer an early form of the urban Gothic genre which would further develop in the fin-de-siècle.

London Expansion and Gothic Discourses of Urbanisation

Amid an unprecedented and astonishing expansion of the metropolis, a new Gothic mode seems perfectly appropriate to engage with the alienation coming not from the past anymore but from the contemporary situation, aligning with Botting's description of the Gothic mode 'as both a repository of the fears of disintegration and the hopes of regaining a sense of unity'.[26] The first half of the nineteenth century indeed came with tremendous social, technological and geographical changes in terms of urbanisation and industrialisation, which London epitomised: 'driven by market forces, it "just growed"'.[27] From about one million inhabitants at the beginning of the century to more than three million by 1860, the city's economic expansion created 'spirals of demand [...]. Baronets, brokers and Bayswater ex-colonials required armies of shop assistants and crossing-sweepers, seamstresses and liveried footmen'.[28] Economic expansion led to more paid work, whether skilled or unskilled, and people from urban areas as well as migrants moved to the metropolis in large numbers in the hopes of benefiting in some way from this overwhelming industrialisation process. The city also profited from colonial expansion as the docks complex developed, which generated employment – though mostly low-paid, day-to-day hiring jobs that were soon outnumbered by the number of candidates. By 1871, a seventh of the total population of England and Wales lived in London.

The capital's rapid growth gave rise to discourses of urbanisation with vivid Gothic undertones, which often ascribed agency to the metropolis as an entity developing of its own accord rather than being developed by people. London was surrounded by vast patches of cheap land, which allowed for a relatively easy expansion. Contrary to such cities as Paris that were geographically constrained to remain within a certain area, London could expand in a rather scattered and irregular way; and so, 'able to spread, London did'.[29] This incoherent development was quickly assimilated to a sort of organic growth, naturally evolving (it was, after all, the century of Charles Darwin's theories of evolutionary biology) outside of humanity's control rather than systematic and organised. Numerous figures of speech used in public discourse betray a sense of London being active in its own development rather than being developed: Henry Mayhew, looking down at the 'leviathan Metropolis' from a hot-air balloon in 1852, declared it impossible to 'tell where the monster city began or ended, for the buildings stretched not only to the horizon on either side, but far away into the distance [...] where the town seemed to blend into the sky'.[30] The personified entities 'the metropolis', 'the city' and 'the town' along with the active voice reveal a sense of threat associated to this potential agency, confirmed by the metropolis's association with the mythical Leviathan. The monster city 'sprawled on',[31] and although the verb can be understood in the modern sense of urban sprawl, i.e. unrestricted and uneven growth regarded as unsustainable due to its lack of consideration for urban planning,[32] it also carries Gothic potential through its negative connotations which echo the term 'monster'. To sprawl is in turn defined as 'to move the limbs in a convulsive effort or struggle', 'to be stretched out in an ungainly or awkward manner', 'to crawl from one place to another in a struggling or ungraceful manner'[33] – the choice of this verb, which comes back often in descriptions of nineteenth-century London, underscores the sense of threat as well as of helplessness in front of this phenomenon. The journalist George Rose Emerson, commenting on suburban progress in the early 1860s, confirms this sense of portending evil in describing that 'now, as we look Londonwards, we find that the metropolis has thrown out its arms and embraced us, not yet with a stifling clutch, but with ominous closeness'.[34]

The city's monstrous arms embracing and trapping its inhabitants while not stifling them 'yet' comes with a sense of foreboding that triggers horror and thrill. 'A great, hungry sea, which flows on and on, [...] and then overspreads its borders, flooding the plains beyond',[35] 'this octopus of London [...] a vast irregular growth',[36] 'a vortex'[37] – the list of nature-related, disquieting images and metaphors used to designate nineteenth-century London goes on.

The extensive and rapid expansion of the metropolis led to a rising cultural anxiety of urbanisation, as a new consciousness of the city as inexplicable and uncontrollable develops. 'The metropolis was too big, it had no soul', Roy Porter describes,[38] and while this vision of a soulless entity certainly feeds into the Gothic image of the city, it can also be read as growing concern about anonymity and the potential loss of identity in the city's vortex. Already in the eighteenth century, London was described as 'constantly suck[ing] in people',[39] and popular culture quickly became rife with stories such as William Hogarth's series of engravings *A Harlot's Progress* (1732): young and/or hopeful people leaving the countryside for the opportunities of the city, never to be heard of again. In 1850, in his *Prelude*'s Book VII dedicated to his time residing in London, William Wordsworth described 'that huge fermenting mass of human-kind' and exclaimed: 'The face of every one / That passes by me is a mystery!'[40] Wordsworth's formulation resorts once more to a threatening, organic analogy to render the crowd and its potential to absorb its inhabitants and turn their individualities into a uniform, anonymous mass. The circulation and anonymization of people along with the constant, seemingly untamed growth of the metropolis therefore provided the perfect frame for a resurgence of the Gothic, to help process and address the cultural anxieties and feelings of oppression, threat and entrapment triggered by the advancing urbanisation.

'The Mysteries of' as an Urban Gothic Genre

Anxieties linked to fast-developing urbanisation and industrialisation and the growing unfamiliarity of the city led to the rise of more specifically urban literary genres as well as to the urbanisation of previously existing trends, as popular culture and literature evolved with the population. James underlines the generational shift that leads to new directions in popular culture: as 'the workers drawn into the cities were being superseded by generations that had known nothing but urban life [...] amid the sprawling jungles of back-to-backs and crowded tenements [...] Their literature became informed by new outlooks and the new idiom of urban drama, song, newspapers, and criminal slang'.[41] With a nod once more to the organic metaphors making sense of the growing city and its potential dangers, James shows that popular culture expanded along with population growth and with the new generations of urban people for whom city life, with all its splendour and all its squalor, constituted normality. This is made manifest by the rise of the so-called city mysteries genre, a popular fiction response to this urbanisation phenomenon.

The 'city mysteries' or 'urban mysteries' form a genre of popular novels that had its heyday in the 1840s and 1850s, and Eugène Sue's 1842 *Mystères de Paris* is usually located at its root, almost as a blueprint of the genre to which G. W. M. Reynolds's *The Mysteries of London* (1844–1845) belongs. In fact, Reynolds's text, like Sue's, is often considered another 'point of imitation' for the genre of the urban novel.[42] The genre showed urban life 'with all its activities and classes of society, as an organic whole'[43] in which characters explore the city's underworld both literally and metaphorically, as crime and deviance are often connected to the underground in an early urban Gothic mode.[44] Contrary to most British penny fiction, the 'city mysteries' were rarely published anonymously; and these *romans-feuilletons* quickly assumed a transnational aspect as they circulated on an international scale through the proliferation of numerous translations, pirated versions or parodies throughout Europe as well as in the United States. They flourished in numerous languages, centring on various cities, including *Les Vrais Mystères de Paris* (1844) by Eugène François Vidocq, *Die Mysterien von Berlin* (1844) by August Brass, *De Verborgenheden van Amsterdam* (1844) by L. van Eikenhorst, *Los Misterios del Plata* (1846) by Juana Manso, *The Mysteries of Lisbon* (1854) by Camilo Castelo Branco, *Les Mystères de Marseille* (1867) by Émile Zola, *I Misteri di Napoli* (1869) by Francesco Mastriani – the list goes on. It is worth noting that the genre remained popular across the European continent for a little longer than it did in the United Kingdom, where it mostly crops us from the mid-1830s to the mid-1850s, which corresponds to what Anne Humpherys points out as the 'consolidation of economic and political power in the big cities, especially London' as the modern city itself and its institutional structures become visible.[45] Given that the genre's popularity was directly dependent on people making sense of growing urbanisation and on the modern city becoming unavoidable, it is no wonder that different countries saw it become popular in different years or even decades, depending on the development of their own urbanising cities.

The 'city mysteries' genre was one way for popular literature to negotiate the confusingly fast-paced changes occurring on all levels of daily life for vast numbers of people. Humpherys convincingly argues that the term 'mysteries' does not merely refer to a plot device, but 'refers linguistically to the fragmented and hence incoherent experience of the modern city as well as to the resulting feelings of disconnectedness'.[46] Instead of focusing on bringing back a certain form of order, the 'mysteries' novel therefore engages with the Gothic concepts of fragmentation and disorder, diffusing the Gothic through the city's urbanity. Though typically associated with the fin-de-siècle thanks to such iconic works as R. L. Stevenson's *Strange Case of Dr Jekyll and Mr Hyde* (1886), urban Gothic is characterised by its attempt to process anxieties of urbanisation and industrialisation by transferring the usual and expected Gothic settings from a rural environment to the city, and is therefore a key feature of earlier texts such as the city mysteries and many penny bloods. Botting describes how in the urban Gothic genre, 'the dark alleyways of cities were the gloomy forests and subterranean labyrinths; criminals were the new villains, cunning, corrupt but thoroughly human'[47] – a transfer which occurs in many plotlines of *The Mysteries of London*. While the formulaic title 'The Mysteries of [...]' echoes Ann Radcliffe's *The Mysteries of Udolpho* (1794), Robert Mighall warns that considering *The Mysteries of London* as a 'mere transplanting of the Radcliffean tale of terror in a modern urban context' would be erroneous,[48] as the genre managed to encompass both a certain urbanisation of more traditional, eighteenth-century Gothic and a fresh consciousness of the modern city as unfathomable and impenetrable. 'This is not just a Gothic in the city, it is a Gothic *of* the city', in Mighall's own terms, as the terrors of the genre firmly belong to the urban experience.[49] Gothic tropes therefore do not become reused per se but rather are fragmented and propagated through the fictional city. Classic and expected plot devices assume new depths as they use the urban experience to challenge the status quo and its novel institutions, most often by looking at the relationship between urbanisation and the lower classes. For instance, instead of the prototypical Gothic villain, 'we get the carceral functioning of the law, the rapaciousness of the financial sector, and the brutality of social services' or a fragmentation of the villain into several characters whose limited power stems from their institutional position.[50] As for the eighteenth-century innocent and persecuted young maiden, she has now become 'split into a variety of victims; in fact the victim can be anyone in the city',[51] as even the damsel in distress loses her identity in the crowd. In terms of setting, Reynolds's *Mysteries* could be described as trading vaults for slums, which results in a less localised and less contained Gothic in the context of the city, thereby more threatening: Gothic energy is diffused through the city's urbanity and through its institutions, rather than focused into one traditional haunted house, castle or monastery. The impact of the Gothic is therefore magnified and woven into a different pattern, which Humpherys describes in the following way: 'the energies which in the gothic building circulate through various internal arteries – hidden rooms, trap doors, and secret passageways – escape into the larger society through a labyrinth of city streets, neighbourhoods, and multi-purpose buildings'.[52] This is not to say that *The Mysteries of London* does not feature said hidden rooms, trap doors and secret passageways, of course, but Humpherys visualises them as a step in the journey of these 'energies', which, not content with circulating in the 'arteries' of a building and therefore giving it life, seem to deploy even stronger agency as they escape into the city, into a labyrinth of institutions and urbanised, maze-like spaces.

The maze-like setting of *The Mysteries of London* has a literal meaning, as it attempts to describe the actual topography of the metropolis which keeps on expanding in an erratic, irregular way. But it is also a figurative maze, as the story's 'labyrinthine narrative'[53] seems driven by teleological reasons on the level of diegesis: the narrator mentioning 'the reader who follows us through the mazes of our narrative' suggests that there is a precise path that readers are following with the narrator amid this maze.[54] The terms 'labyrinth' and 'maze' must be defined and contrasted, here: although a common definition exists as 'a structure consisting in a complex network of paths' and purposefully 'designed as a puzzle', a distinction can be made as well.[55] Indeed, a labyrinth can be defined as 'consisting only of one convoluted path to the centre and back, rather than containing a number of dead ends' and thus analysed as a somewhat guiding path, albeit complex and dizzying, which always leads one to its centre and/or back out. A maze, on the other hand, presents numerous options to choose from, and it is possible to choose wrongly and face repeated dead ends, with no guarantee to ever find either the way through or the way back. Both terms are often used interchangeably, and Mighall is right in calling the *Mysteries of London* narrative itself 'labyrinthine',[56] for the reader is undoubtedly guided through the story in a convoluted but goal-driven way. However, I will favour 'maze' when addressing how the city is presented on the level of diegesis, because of its more threatening Gothic potential.

A Moral and Material Maze: Urbanising the Gothic in Penny Bloods

The motif of the urban Gothic maze is not exclusive to the city mysteries genre. With popular fiction conditioned by new urban city life, the use of this motif was one way to Gothicise the city in 1830s–1850s popular literature – Charles Dickens's *Oliver Twist* (1837–1839) is an early example of the use of the urban Gothic mode through the depiction of the metropolis as a maze, though in a realist work. Such an image was a direct reaction to the waves of shock triggered by city expansion, as it worked 'against the sense that modern urban life ha[d] coherent meaning'.[57] Penny bloods, often a way to help the lower classes address their own contemporary context, contributed to the development of this trope by characterising the growing metropolis as an urban Gothic maze within their diegesis. *The String of Pearls* is a telling example: narrow streets and dark alleyways as well as underground tunnels constitute part of the décor of the story, particularly in connection with the murderous enterprise ran by Sweeney Todd and Mrs Lovett. Furthermore, Todd's barbershop is located on Fleet Street and Mrs Lovett's pie shop in Bell Yard, just round the corner. This spot is particularly noteworthy as it coincides with the original site of Temple Bar (where Fleet Street now meets the Strand on a modern map) which, until 1878, marked the boundary between London and Westminster, and was one of the busiest entrances to the City of London. The fact that Todd murders his victims almost exactly at the place that represents the city's border hints at the quasi-sacrificial nature of these murders, as a rite of passage which, as Victor Turner argues, could potentially enable experimentation with alternative social relations.[58] This point of entry can therefore be analysed as enabling Todd's experimentation with a reversal of the social order, with 'those above [serving] those down below', to quote lyrics from the modern musical adaptation of the story.[59] The quasi-sacrificial aspect of these murders also contributes to the city's representation as a maze as it echoes the ancient myth of the Minotaur, to whom young Athenians would regularly be sacrificed by being sent into the Cretan labyrinth that harboured the creature. Entering the labyrinth sealed the fate of the victims as it condemned them to a certain monstrous death – just like Todd's customers' fate was often sealed once they entered the Fleet Street barber shop. In this penny blood, the metropolis is both the labyrinth and the monster: the story reacts to the topical cultural anxiety of fast-developing urbanisation and its unprecedented sense of anonymity by making literal the threat of being 'swallowed up' the very moment one enters the boundaries of London. By depicting people who lose their bodies as well as their identities, rather than merely losing touch with their loved ones, this cannibalistic cautionary folktale builds on the image of the urban Gothic maze by suggesting several levels, literal as well as metaphorical.

The daze induced by the unfamiliarity and potential confusion stemming from modern city life translates into the development of several other characteristics of urban Gothic in penny bloods, beyond that of the Gothic maze. For instance, the Gothic grows chronologically closer, as penny bloods already establish what Alison Milbank considers a 'novel feature of *later* Victorian Gothic[:] its contemporary and localized setting in the Britain of its own century'.[60] Two key aspects of Milbank's statement can be identified in 1840s penny bloods and show a certain internalisation of the Gothic: the contemporary and the localized. In terms of period, Reynolds's *The Mysteries of London* is suggested as taking place at a time that is contemporary to its publication. *The String of Pearls* is not, but is presented as beginning 'when George the Third was young', thus placing the story less than a century away from its readership considering that George III reigned from 1760 to 1820.[61] As for the localized British setting, Milbank recognises Reynolds as 'provid[ing] the conditions for an indigenous Gothic site' in Britain along with William Ainsworth's development of topographical Gothic with such novels as *The Tower of London* (1841) and *Windsor Castle* (1843),[62] which stems of course from the contemporary obsession with the city. To underscore the impact of moving the Gothic setting from remote, unidentifiable places to locations the reader will recognise, James quotes a 1916 statement in the *Bootle Times* by an old man who was an avid reader of popular fiction in his youth: 'to my mind', he said, 'the most fascinating part of the old stories was the fact that they often treated of places you knew'.[63] Indeed, a sense of verisimilitude and of proximity was added by the fact that readers were provided with an outstanding number of geographical bearings in some penny bloods. In *The String of Pearls*, virtually every street of London which the characters walk is named, and all the streets and places mentioned actually existed at the time: the main places of the story, Fleet Street (where Sweeney Todd's shop is located), Old St Dunstan's Church and Bell Yard (where Mrs Lovett sells her pies); but also places to which the characters only go once, such as Hyde Park Corner or Peckham Rye. Londoners were thus implicitly invited to imagine Mrs Lovett's pies as they passed Bell Yard, or a subterranean crypt containing human remains under St Dunstan's Church, prolonging the thrill of the story as well as complicating the image of the city they might have had.

The reality of the places featured in the stories gives more weight to some of the themes addressed in the story of Sweeney Todd, too, for instance its distrust of religion. The more obvious sign of this is the use of the character of Reverend Lupin almost exclusively as comic relief, but the urban Gothic mode strengthens this theme via its treatment of St Dunstan's Church. Though most of the action takes place in Todd's shop, it so happens that the final revelation begins in this church, since it is only thanks to its 'strange and most abominable odour' in Chapter 19 that Todd and Lovett's business is finally exposed.[64] The church is thus a key element as far as plot progression is concerned. What is more, the 'positively terrific' odour in the church leads to opening the subterranean crypt[65] – yet another typically Gothic setting here embedded in the city – which communicates with the cellars under both Todd's and Mrs Lovett's shops, linking all the pieces of the puzzle. Therefore, the building with the strongest Gothic quality is the one that also holds the key to the mystery; but instead of being the expected symbol of salvation, the church becomes complicit with the murders. *The String of Pearls* echoes what was common practice in London prior to the 1852 Burial Act and proposes a perverted version of the pre-Victorian cemetery, as burial grounds until the end of the eighteenth century were 'placed at the heart of the city, next to the church' with tombs inside the church and others outside of it.[66] Interment directly beneath metropolitan churches was frequent, and the number of interments performed for a cheap price led to a few sensational cases such as that of Enon Chapel (in Clement's Lane, on the Strand): With the conclusion that at least 12,000 people had been buried there, '[t]he greater part of the earth removed from under Enon Chapel to the Waterloo Road was human bodies in a state of putrefaction', with 'nothing but planking' separating the ground floor of the church and the decomposing bodies.[67] Here, the penny blood proposes another version of this news story, making the church complicit with horrifying, uncanny possibilities. With its 'charnel-house sort of smell', St Dunstan's reeks of dead bodies and becomes a mass grave; and the scent pervades the air in such a powerful way that even the most reasonable people are 'nearly stifled', from the Reverend Joseph Stillingport and the visiting bishop to the organ-player, the churchwardens and churchgoers.[68] The characters' discussion of the stench remains consistent with the treatment of Reverend Lupin in other parts of the story as it ridicules the churchwardens:

> 'Is this horrid charnel-house sort of smell always here?'
> 'I am afraid it is,' said one of the churchwardens.
> 'Afraid!' said the bishop, 'surely you know; you seem to me to have a nose.'
> 'Yes,' said the churchwarden, in great confusion, 'I have that honour, and I have the pleasure of informing you, my lord bishop – I mean I have the honour of informing you, that this smell is always here.'[69]

With a tone that continues to discredit the Church, the situation which is narrated in Chapter 19 also bears a metaphorical dimension which further emphasises a certain mistrust in the city as well as in religion. Even pious, religious men who, in theory, should represent purity and a form of innocence, are contaminated. Metaphorically, the city corrupts even the innocent, as St Dunstan's intolerable stench is 'so bad' that

> some of the congregation were forced to leave, and have been seen to slink into Bell-yard, where Lovett's pie-shop was situated, and then and there relieve themselves with a pork or a veal pie, in order that their mouths and noses should be full of a delightful and agreeable flavour, instead of one most peculiarly and decidedly the reverse.[70]

In other words, the smell of human remains rotting in the crypt ironically drives innocent people to go and consume their fellow humans'/Londoners' flesh in Mrs Lovett's pies, as they try to escape the stench that is in fact produced by the very business they support, in a lugubrious vicious circle. St Dunstan's Church symbolises the fact that city dwellers' bodies as well as their humanity become corrupt as the Gothic city swallows up its inhabitants physically and morally.

As the Gothic becomes urbanised and thus moves closer to readers' daily lives, its subject matter also acquires new depths by centring increasingly on the self. Botting stresses a new focus on interiority in the nineteenth century and explains that 'less identifiable as a separate genre [...], Gothic fiction seemed to go underground: its depths were less romantic chasms or labyrinthine dungeons, than the murky recesses of human subjectivity'.[71] In the context of industrialisation and along with the advancement of science and burgeoning questionings about the human mind, the relationship between the individual and society became a central preoccupation. Botting's 'murky recesses of human subjectivity' refer to both a mysterious quality stemming from a lack of knowledge, and the potential for darkness that lies within the individual. The urban Gothic mode helped express this shift by combining several concerns in its tales, as 'domestic, industrial and urban contexts and aberrant individuals provided the loci for mystery and terror'.[72] This narrower focus, closer to the individual (whether physically or psychologically) in all three contexts, is particularly relevant in terms of the characterisation of the villain(s): Sweeney Todd, for example, is presented to readers as a criminal whose evil actions are not justified through any backstory.[73] He has no motive for murdering customers apart from financial profit, he kills at random, and despite a few ogre-like physical characteristics that add to the horror he inspires, he remains nevertheless a frighteningly normal human being. Like an early Mr Hyde, Todd hints at the threat of moral and social degeneration; but in viewing its customers as merchandise leading to financial profit, he also embodies the threatening potential of capitalism and industrialisation dehumanising people, who become cogs in a machine which takes away individuality. He is, in Botting's words, a typically urban Gothic 'new villain': 'cunning, corrupt but thoroughly human' – that is to say, neither a monster nor a supernatural being, but fallible and terribly ordinary.[74] His evil crimes stem from human decisions, thus confronting the readers with the dark potential of social changes and of human subjectivity.

Whether it is through a strong eighteenth-century-Gothic legacy, like in *Varney the Vampyre*, or through the development of the urban Gothic mode, like in *The Mysteries of London* and *The String of Pearls*, penny bloods markedly demonstrate an appropriation of the Gothic to address contemporary contexts and reflect what Garrett calls 'the central nineteenth-century preoccupation with the relation of self and society'.[75] As human subjectivity and the relation to a fast-changing society become primary concerns, the Gothic allows reflection on contemporary crises as the individual attempts to find and understand its place within this new context. In their use of the Gothic, 1840s penny bloods thus helped their readership negotiate increasingly rapid social change by providing a fictional world in which the various contemporary issues that are in movement meet. Hogle explains the suitability of the Gothic for this purpose as follows:

> What better symbolic mechanism can there be, multidirectional as Gothic figures are, for abjecting betwixt and between, anomalous conditions where opposed positions of many kinds keep blurring into each other and threatening us with the dissolution of our normal cultural foundations for the identities we claim to possess? The Gothic has been and remains necessary to modern western culture because it allows us [...] to confront the roots of our beings in sliding multiplicities (from life becoming death to genders mixing to fear becoming pleasure and more) and to define ourselves against these uncanny abjections, [...] in a kind of cultural activity that as time passes can keep inventively changing its ghosts of counterfeits to address changing psychological and cultural longings and fears.[76]

Employing Julia Kristeva's concept of the abject, as a force drawing one to the 'place where meaning collapses' through the loss of distinction between subject and object, or between self and other,[77] Hogle describes the multidirectional nature of the Gothic as the most suited symbolic mechanism to process and confront changes and 'uncanny abjections'. The very essence of the Gothic makes it the perfect tool to address our 'sliding multiplicities' and adapt to 'changing psychological cultural longings and fears', through a medium which uses its own fictionality to permit a form of experimentation with the new potential threats faced at a precise point in time by a society. This helps explain the continued circulation of the Gothic after its first heyday, and I argue that it also helps to demonstrate the circulation of penny bloods through literary genres. Penny bloods are not Gothic texts per se, but they adopt and appropriate the essence of the Gothic, which Hogle describes above, and thereby played a key part in the development of the early urban Gothic genre.

By selecting and adopting various elements from different literary traditions, penny bloods produce a result that answers the particular needs of a period, be it in terms of format or content. In doing so, they fully exploit two potential meanings of the term 'circulation': its literal meaning as the distribution of periodical publications and their transmission from person to person, but also the figurative meaning of a movement within an established system. As with oral storytelling or sensationalism, the penny bloods' incorporation of the Gothic facilitates their active circulation within the network of late-eighteenth-century and early-nineteenth-century popular literature and culture, through which they create their own place within the frame of the popular.

Notes

1. James, *Fiction for the Working Man*, 77.
2. Ibid.
3. Hogle, 'Gothic in Western Culture', 1.
4. Botting, *Gothic*, 128.
5. Flanders, *Invention of Murder*, 58.
6. Sala qtd. in Flanders, *Invention of Murder*, 22–23.
7. Clery, 'Genesis of "Gothic" Fiction', 21.
8. Maturin qtd. in Miles, 'Effulgence of Gothic', 59; see also Potter 2021.
9. Miles, 'Effulgence of Gothic', 60.
10. Hogle, 'Gothic in Western Culture', 1.
11. James, *Fiction for the Working Man*, 72.
12. Ibid., 73–76.
13. For more about the general technique of scissors-and-paste in penny fiction contexts, see Burz-Labrande and Léger-St-Jean 2023.
14. Ibid., 77.
15. Bleiler, 'Introduction', 784.
16. James, *Fiction for the Working Man*, 89.
17. Garrett, *Gothic Reflections*, 1.
18. Ibid., 1–2.
19. See for instance Humpherys and James 2008; Conary and Shannon 2023.
20. Potter, *History of Gothic Publishing*, 2, 1.
21. James, *Fiction for the Working Man*, 78–79.
22. Rymer, *Varney, the Vampire*, 35.
23. Collins Jenkins, *Vampire Forensics*, 69; see also Frayling 1992.
24. James, *Fiction for the Working Man*, 85.
25. Hogle, 'Gothic in Western Culture', 3.
26. Botting, *Gothic*, 128.
27. Porter, *London: A Social History*, 226.
28. Ibid.
29. Ibid., 251.
30. Mayhew, 'Balloon View of London', 9.
31. Porter, *London: A Social History*, 226.
32. Batty et al., 'Suburban Sprawl', 1.
33. Oxford English Dictionary, s.v. 'sprawl', accessed 27 March 2025, http://www.oed.com/view/Entry/187618.
34. Emerson qtd. in Porter, *London: A Social History*, 267.
35. Sherwell, *Life in West London*, 2.
36. Geddes, *Cities in Evolution*, 26.
37. Llewelyn Smith qtd. in Banks, 'The Contagion of Numbers', 112.

38 Porter, *London: A Social History*, 340.
39 Harris, *England in the 18th Century*, 5.
40 Wordsworth, 'Book VII', 197.
41 James, *Fiction for the Working Man*, 146.
42 Humpherys, 'Generic Strands', 456.
43 James, *Fiction for the Working Man*, 156.
44 See Raine 2021.
45 Humpherys, 'Generic Strands', 456.
46 Ibid.
47 Botting, *Gothic*, 123.
48 Mighall, *Geography of Victorian Gothic*, 30.
49 Ibid.; emphasis original.
50 Humpherys, 'Generic Strands', 457–458.
51 Ibid., 458.
52 Ibid., 459.
53 Mighall, *Geography of Victorian Gothic*, 31.
54 Reynolds, *Mysteries of London*, 206.
55 Oxford English Dictionary, s.v. 'labyrinth' and 'maze', accessed 27 March 2025, http://www.oed.com/view/Entry/104763; http://www.oed.com/view/Entry/115347.
56 Mighall, *Geography of Victorian Gothic*, 31.
57 Humpherys, 'Geometry of the Modern City', 76.
58 Turner, *Ritual Process*, 96.
59 Sondheim and Wheeler, *Sweeney Todd*, 86.
60 Milbank, 'Victorian Gothic', 147; emphasis original.
61 'The String of Pearls', 3.
62 Milbank, 'Victorian Gothic', 149.
63 *Bootle Times*, 'Old Boys' Periodicals', 8.
64 'The String of Pearls', 149.
65 Ibid., 151.
66 Foucault, 'Of Other Spaces', 25.
67 *Reports from Select Committees*, 231.
68 'The String of Pearls', 149, 150.
69 Ibid., 153.
70 Ibid., 151.
71 Botting, *Gothic*, 11.
72 Ibid., 123.
73 Contrary to later adaptations and rewritings of the tale in popular culture – see Labrande 2020.
74 Ibid.
75 Garrett, *Gothic Reflections*, 3.
76 Hogle, 'Gothic in Western Culture', 16–17.
77 Kristeva, *Powers of Horror*, 2.

Chapter 4

CONSUMING THE PENNY DREADFUL IN NEO-VICTORIAN FICTION

The circulation of penny bloods and penny dreadfuls during the Victorian period amid the marketplace as well as popular genres shows that penny publications are in constant movement over the course of the nineteenth century, always circulated further. Sweeney Todd's transmedial journey as a character, from early Victorian times all the way to the twenty-first century, confirms that penny publications can also circulate efficiently through different media as well as across different epochs: from George Dibdin Pitt's instantaneous stage version motivated by commercial and political interests in 1847, to Stephen Sondheim's musical (premiering in 1979) and Tim Burton's movie adaption (2007) developing the character's tragedy on stage and screen, and back to the page, with the redeeming power of neo-Victorianism in Terry Pratchett's *Dodger* (2012), the material and its content adapt and take on different forms in order to remain relevant.[1] But in addition to these forms of dissemination, other more or less direct references to penny bloods and penny dreadfuls begin to circulate and multiply within recent neo-Victorian fiction narratives, too; interestingly, this often occurs in genre fiction works with a popular appeal and published in a series format, which echoes the penny dreadful's own publication context. From the use of the phrase 'penny dreadful' to the resurrection of penny dreadful characters, these appearances function within neo-Victorianism's critical engagement with the Victorian past,[2] and together, form an emerging additional pattern of circulation of penny dreadfuls which culminates into their establishment as a cultural reference.

The Penny Dreadful Name

Though the publications do not form part of the main plots, various mentions of penny bloods or penny dreadfuls appear in recent neo-Victorian fiction (with varying frequency from one work to the next), fulfilling different functions in the narratives. The most famous recent instance is undoubtedly the television series *Penny Dreadful* (2014–2016), which brought the phrase back into cultural knowledge and made it famous on a global scale. Created by John Logan, the series is a mash-up of familiar eighteenth- and nineteenth-century literary characters, whose omnipresent intertextuality has been extensively studied.[3] However, penny dreadfuls are only directly mentioned once throughout the series, which is certainly not an adaptation or a revisitation of the phenomenon. Instead, it pays tribute to its namesake through other strategies: the choice of the phrase as a title along with a serialized format that does not rely strongly on teleology, a patchwork approach to building plotlines and a reliance on audience engagement for marketing purposes[4] together constitute an echo to the penny dreadful's status as a key cultural text of the popular and to its forms of entertainment.

In other neo-Victorian examples, the use of the phrase refers directly to the original penny publications. In *The Way of All Flesh* (2018) by Ambrose Parry, the single reference to penny dreadfuls resuscitates the long-standing criticism about the publications' sensationalism and supposed amorality. As the characters discuss a recent murder, Mina, the sister of Dr Simpson's wife, is described as 'sp[eaking] with ill-disguised fascination about this poor girl's gruesome fate, as though she were reading from a penny dreadful'.[5] Though seemingly a passing comment, the implications are crucial for the characterisation of Mina. She does not belong to the typical imagined audience of the original penny dreadful, in that she is neither particularly young nor a member of the working-class; however, she is still dangerously close to standing at the margins of society, as spinsterhood looms over her future. She participates actively in the circulation of gossip, fascinated by 'vicarious excitement and scandal' rather than concerning herself with the role she is expected to fulfil,[6] that of a meek woman whose life should be dedicated to her own (either current or future) household and to charitable work – a role which the enjoyment of penny dreadfuls comes to disturb. At the same time, this reference is consistent with the characterisation of Will Raven, whose internal focalisation we read in these lines. When the story opens, Will lives in a 'lodging house that was among the cheapest in the town; just above the workhouse in terms of comfort', in the Old Town of Edinburgh, the underworld of the city.[7] He is poor, in debt, and knows this part of the city well – but he has a liminal position, too, as a medical student who is hired by Dr Simpson and moves among other spheres of society. The description he makes of Mina is informed by this position: the reader, while not knowing whether Mina has ever read a penny dreadful herself, can trust that Will surely has encountered these publications; and Will locates Mina at the margins with a single phrase, relying on how much it clashes with her social rank. As a result, this phrase is used as a code for certain characteristics; and while this necessitates the reader's understanding and knowledge of the phrase, *The Way of All Flesh* remains on the safe side by coupling it with the periphrasis 'with ill-disguised fascination' to ensure its readers understand the full implications of the use of the phrase 'penny dreadful'.

Another neo-Victorian novel, E. S. Thomson's *Beloved Poison* (2016), seemingly refers to penny bloods in a similar way, but uses such direct mentions in order to bring nuance to, or even challenge, discourses of criticism of penny dreadfuls and to present a lower-class perspective. The story, set in 1846 (i.e. after the first wave of the extremely successful *Mysteries of London*, and amidst the publication of both *The String of Pearls* and *Varney the Vampyre*), features Jem Lockhart, an apprentice apothecary in the fictional St Saviour's Infirmary in London, built in 1135 and soon to be demolished. When six small coffins are discovered, each containing dried flowers and bundles of rags, Jem begins to investigate with the help of Will Quartermain, the junior architect in charge of emptying the graveyard ahead of the demolition. The novel itself contains numerous elements reminiscent of a penny blood (although its storyline is teleological): murder in the underbelly of the city, questions of bodysnatching, a cross-dressing protagonist and a potential ghost (or killer) called the Abbot. As Jem tells Will,

> St Saviour's is ancient. It was here during the Black Death, the Reformation, the Civil War. Can you not imagine a Protestant martyr burned alive, who cannot rest? A medieval prior done to death by drowning in mead? Did you never read the penny bloods when you were younger?[8]

From the first chapter, the link to penny bloods is drawn and the mystery already opens with a strong Gothic potential, as Jem mentions stories of spirits haunting the infirmary. Once setting and plot have been established, Will becomes the reader's spokesperson, as his answer to Jem – 'Go on then. Entertain me!'[9] – highlights the primary function of these narratives, as the story properly begins. Jem's answer, in turn, introduces the contemporary criticism of penny bloods being the 'wrong' kind of reading material: '[My father] used to throw my penny bloods onto the fire. He does the same to Gabriel's – that's until I told the lad where to hide them'.[10] While the father seems to represent the contemporary discourses of criticism, Jem is both a reader and a defender of the entertaining quality of penny bloods, and as a departure from her father and his own discourse, she helps the young apprentice Gabriel keep his own penny bloods. The war over cheap publications and the suitability of the reading material they offer is further referred to later in the novel, in a scene that makes clear which position is taken by the text. When the protagonists go to a brothel to obtain information from the owner Mrs Roseplucker, two young prostitutes are present in the room, lying on a sofa and looking bored. What they are doing, however, is of particular interest: 'Both held a pamphlet. One had folded hers into the shape of a bird, the other [...] was using hers to fan her face'.[11] This use of pamphlets could of course mean that the two characters are simply illiterate and thus find a use for the pages they cannot read. But Mrs Roseplucker can read, and when Jem picks up one of her penny bloods and throws it back onto the floor, Mrs Roseplucker stares at her 'with malevolent eyes'.[12] If her girls are allowed to fold and destroy pamphlets for their own amusement, but her penny bloods are not to be touched, then it is clear that the pamphlets have already been dismissed by the mistress of the house. This echoes the rise of the Society for the Diffusion of Useful Knowledge (SDUK) in the 1840s and the publication of penny pamphlets aimed at providing reading material to the poor and at guiding them towards the supposedly right sort of literature. This brothel scene can be read as displaying the failed attempts of higher classes to exert control over the lower classes during this period of growing literacy (the poor response to improvement pamphlets leading to the disbandment of the SDUK soon after),[13] as well as stressing the agency the lower classes preserved in choosing their own reading material.

Mrs Roseplucker herself is presented as an avid reader of penny bloods. In fact, they become an integral part of her characterisation as she is hardly ever seen without an instalment in hand: 'She was reading a greasy, well-thumbed copy of *Crimes of Old London*', 'staring at me accusingly over the top of her penny blood', 'her dog-eared copy of *The Vampyre Returns*', 'She pocketed the coins and turned back to her penny blood'[14] – the list goes on. When she finally agrees to tell Jem and Will more about the infirmary, she launches into a retelling of a ghostly tale in an 'adaptation [...] vividly coloured by the bloodthirsty realism of Reynolds' [sic] Penny Weeklies'.[15] Not only does Mrs Roseplucker read penny bloods, but she also seems to be able to tell them – a fact that echoes the oral storytelling tradition but also foreshadows the revelation later made in the third volume of Thomson's series, *The Blood* (2018), that she is a penny blood author herself. In this light, the description of Mrs Roseplucker and her environment takes on more significance. At first, it seems to feed once again into the heavy criticism of penny bloods and their consequences at the time:

> Mrs Roseplucker was sitting beside the fire. [...] Her lips moved soundlessly as she turned the page of a greasy-looking penny blood. Beside her chair more of the same were scattered: *Ramona and the Bloody Hand*; *Dick of Old London*; *Lady Elvira's Secret*. [...] [T]he daylight revealed a slovenly domesticity, the dusty mantel, the threadbare furnishings, a chipped plate of congealed kipper bones on the hearth.[16]

This description recalls the character of Betsy in the Mayhew brothers' *The Greatest Plague Of Life: or, The Adventures Of A Lady In Search Of A Good Servant* (1847). In this satirical fiction, Betsy, the maid addicted to 'trumpery penny novels', reads for hours and is surrounded by penny issues that lie on the floor of the kitchen that she does not have time to clean, 'for what did *she* care about the fish or the potatoes so long as she could have a quiet half-hour's cry over the "Black Pirate"'.[17] The echo created by the picture painted in *Beloved Poison* further highlights the association between penny blood reading and dirt and/ or dishonour – both because of Mrs Roseplucker's professional activity, and because penny bloods are here directly associated with either grease, dirt, or a more generally unkempt state. It must be noted, however, that though middle-class critics would likely place the two women on a similar level, their stories operate differently: Betsy is a maid in a respectable house, and her story expresses the societal disorder fantasised by the contemporary higher classes.[18] Mrs Roseplucker owns a brothel, in a neo-Victorian story which creates spaces to reflect on and critically engage with the Victorian past.

The encounter with Mrs Roseplucker and her reading habit creates the perfect setting for the protagonist to challenge stereotypes associated with the Victorian era. When Jem picks up a penny blood and leafs through it, its plot gives rise to strikingly modern considerations:

> I plucked Lady Elvira from the wreckage and flicked through its pages. The story of a wealthy heiress locked away in an asylum while her fortune was squandered by a theatrically nefarious husband, it had kept Gabriel enthralled for weeks. But I knew for certain that there were far more men than 'ladies' shut up in asylums. [...] For every wrongly imprisoned heiress or pregnant unwed girl locked away there were a hundred broken down fathers weeping or raving beside them. I could guess which version of events fiction – and posterity – would choose to remember.[19]

Jem, cross-dressed as a man, is trained as an apothecary, and the reader is therefore led to trust this statement aimed to set the record straight about asylums. Through this, Thomson ensures that her readership's potential stereotypes about the time are corrected – or at least questioned.[20] The meeting with Mrs Roseplucker provides the setting necessary to allow the text to challenge gender clichés still held about the Victorian era. By using penny bloods and by hinting at the Gothic tradition in which they inscribe themselves (with a plot reminiscent of eighteenth-century Gothic centring on inheritance, a woman locked away, a 'theatrically nefarious husband'), Thomson's novel provides its protagonist Jem with the opportunity to spotlight the gendered double standard which led to such stereotypes. Jem reflects upon the reality of asylums in early Victorian times, and the emphasis on the phrase 'and posterity' using en-dashes functions like an aside from the author to the readers, who have the hindsight that Jem cannot have and can verify the claim against their own preconceived notions. The use of the phrase 'choose to remember' rather than simply 'remember' also involves more agency and decision power, to further emphasise how what is left for posterity about a period such as the Victorian era is a result from choices which fed into this gendered double standard, and which should be challenged and questioned. The scene at Mrs Roseplucker's and the direct involvement of penny bloods thus reveal an authorial intention to make readers of neo-Victorian fiction engage with the past in a more critical fashion.

My penultimate example, *Strange Practice* (2017) by Vivian Shaw, also includes several direct mentions of penny dreadfuls (referring to penny bloods, in terms of chronology), which this time do not replicate nineteenth-century criticism discourses at all but rather turns them upside down. *Strange Practice* is the first volume of Shaw's Dr Greta Helsing novels. Greta has taken up her father's medical practice in present-day London and caters to a patient base which, as she puts it, 'to the majority of the population did not, technically, when you got right down to it, exist': she treats the 'differently alive' and practices 'supernatural medicine', and Greta's patients can 'largely be classified under the heading of monstrous – in its descriptive, rather than pejorative, sense: vampires, were-creatures, mummies, banshees, ghouls, bogey-men, the occasional arthritic barrow-wight. She herself was solidly and entirely human'.[21] In this context, when asked about whether she has ever read *Varney the Vampyre*, she answers that 'she's read practically all the horror classics, well-known and otherwise, for research purposes'.[22] In her hands, penny dreadfuls become sources of information and of knowledge, even scholarship on the creatures that Greta treats. She studies them and relies on them, and by labelling them 'classics', she relocates them at the opposite end of the literature spectrum and makes these texts, which have never been granted access to the literary canon, part of a counter-canon.

The new status of penny dreadfuls as an accepted form of knowledge thus endows Greta with power in Foucauldian terms, and reverses the power dynamics at play in their rejection. This twist gives the long-criticised penny dreadfuls a new dimension and almost attempts to redeem them, though in a world with supernatural creatures, proposing a fictional alternate reality in which they are regarded as useful and informational rather than decried as 'wastes of print'.[23] Such a perspectival shift is what makes this novel decidedly neo-Victorian, despite its twenty-first-century setting. The novel also contains a few rather tongue-in-cheek indirect references to penny bloods, as Greta offers Varney 'amusing if unimproving literature' to keep busy.[24] She later dismisses a potential romantic relationship by pointing out her 'noticeable lack of lacy nightgowns and swooning' and that he is 'known to go for the sort of lady who clutches the bedclothes to her snowy bosom and quavers "the vampyre, the vampyre" through bloodless lips',[25] in an echo to eighteenth-century Gothic female characters as well as to the first scene of *Varney the Vampyre*. While these more indirect intertextual references function as winks to the part of Shaw's readership already familiar with penny dreadfuls, it is primarily the direct references mentioned above that show another step taken in the diachronic circulation of penny bloods and penny dreadfuls.

Reviving Penny Blood Characters

Direct mentions of penny bloods or penny dreadfuls are not the only way in which these publications circulate in neo-Victorian fiction, as penny blood characters have now started to join the fictional world of neo-Victorianism in literature. Sweeney Todd is a prime example, and the various aspects of the character's transmedial circulation from the page to the stage to the screen and back to the page have been extensively analysed.[26] But recent neo-Victorian fiction has now turned to reviving other penny blood characters, such as Sir Francis Varney. Despite its success and major influence on the development of vampire fiction, *Varney the Vampyre* or its protagonist have so far very rarely been brought back into twenty-first-century popular culture. In the *Penny Dreadful* TV series (season 1 episode 6), the penny blood is briefly mentioned when Van Helsing gives one of its instalments to Dr Frankenstein, but it only serves to allow the two characters to discuss the blood-drinking creature they really are after. Further sporadic references to *Varney the Vampyre* can be spotted in other filmic or written works, but these tend to function merely as shorthand for Gothic fiction rather than reviving the original penny blood or its eponymous character. By contrast, in Vivian Shaw's *Strange Practice*, Sir Francis Varney plays a major part as one the main characters who helps bring about the plot's resolution.

Intertextuality runs through the entire novel and is established in its very premise. The name of the protagonist herself, Greta Helsing, echoes Bram Stoker's Professor Abraham Van Helsing, and the novel explains this through the naturalisation of the family after its arrival in Britain: 'the Helsing family [...] dropped the van from their name in the 1930s, fleeing the Netherlands ahead of the gathering storm of WWII' and made 'a transition from hunters to simply scholars'.[27] Although Greta is descended from Van Helsing, she could hardly be more different: he is male and old, she is female and thirty-four; he fought supernatural creatures, she heals them. Shaw provides a modern take on the nineteenth-century character by developing a present-day Helsing, who is less governed by fear and more informed – but also more compassionate and interested in understanding. The gender reversal operated here is not innocent: the bearer of knowledge and of science is now a young woman who runs her own business and has proven her skills, instead of a belligerent, old man admired by a patriarchal society. When London is threatened by a sect of murderous monks who kill both humans and non-humans, Greta endeavours to investigate, with the help of a few supernatural friends such as Varney and Lord Ruthven, protagonist of John Polidori's *The Vampyre* (1819). Interestingly, these are two founding characters of vampire fiction and the ones that contributed most directly to the development of Stoker's Count Dracula and to the modern idea of the vampire.[28] Rather than remaining villains, like in their original stories, in Shaw's story Varney and Ruthven become heroes, and they are both indispensable to the resolution of the plot. In this case, both vampires are the perfect neo-Victorian villains as theorised by Benjamin Poore, in that they are 'migratory creatures' who 'cross over from their allotted narratives and acquire a different narrative function in someone else's story, refusing to "stay put" or "know their place" in time and space'.[29] In *Strange Practice*, Shaw allows them to refuse to 'stay put' as villains and helps them acquire the very different narrative function that Poore mentions. The refusal to 'know their place' in time and space is rendered particularly relevant by their very nature as vampires, too, as their place in cultural memory and folklore is challenged and ever-expanded by such diachronic circulation: Varney as a character keeps circulating and invades the twenty-first century, refusing to meet his end at the close of his original penny blood and to obey a teleological structure.

The novel displays a strong sense of self-reflexivity about its intertextuality and about what it does to its main characters (or what it allows them to do). In addition to the direct mentions of penny dreadfuls and their status shift as a knowledge source, the characters show a certain awareness of the fact that they echo previous literary or cultural works. Even before Sir Francis Varney enters the narrative, Lord Ruthven and Greta explicitly discuss Polidori's novel as libel, and they address the difference in spelling between 'vampire' and 'vampyre', defining categories in vampire taxonomy which allow the characters to give readers a glimpse of the history of vampire fiction. There are other references to the evolution of the character of the vampire, too, for instance when Ruthven tells Greta: 'You know perfectly well I don't burst into flames in sunlight. That bit didn't come along until Murnau in 1922', referring to the silent film *Nosferatu* directed by Friedrich Murnau in 1922, now considered the first vampire movie.[30] Through these intertextual references introduced with humour, the collective image of the vampire is being investigated and deconstructed, both in content and in form. In terms of characterisation, the two vampires in *Strange Practice* undergo a very different treatment which seems to point at their respective status in contemporary popular culture. Ruthven's original characteristics from Polidori's text do feature in Shaw's narrative, such as his strength, his fortune, his social status and some physical traits, but he is also decidedly modernised for comic effect. According to Greta, he 'didn't go in for your standard-variety vampire angst'; he drives, makes tiramisu and has bouts of depression in the winter.[31] The fact that he is revamped, presented as having adopted twenty-first-century hobbies (such as latte art) as well as undergoing a decidedly modern psychologisation, is introduced humorously to create a stronger contrast with his original version – which the text can afford precisely *because* he is a more well-known fictional character. By contrast, Sir Francis Varney is described in greater detail in Shaw's novel and always in ways that are consistent with the original penny blood. From his type of dentition to his eyes 'famously described as "polished tin"',[32] which is indeed the exact phrasing used in the penny blood,[33] Varney himself seems straight out of his source text. The original penny blood character also introduced the idea of the sympathetic vampire, that is to say, a vampire who elicits sympathy through the fact that he is aware of his condition, a slave to his own vampirism, and suffers from it. This self-awareness is reflected in *Strange Practice* too, as he appears depressed, every chapter narrated by him full of self-loathing and regret. In the first half of the novel, Varney sees his own wretched life as follows:

> 'One thing I have learned beyond the shadow of a doubt throughout my existence is that anything that can possibly go wrong will go wrong.' […] It was one of the first things he had really come to understand about his half-existence, in the early years; it explained why everything he ever attempted to achieve had ended up the same way, at the point of a sword, the tines of a pitchfork, the flames of a torch.[34]

In having Varney view his life as essentially the oldest iteration of Murphy's law, Shaw renders his desperation humorous for the readers, who laugh at the expense of the vampire while pitying him. This summary of the original penny blood's many plot twists and resurrections – along with Varney's lamenting – then becomes challenged regularly as the plot of Shaw's novel unfolds. When Varney struggles to understand why a human would help cure creatures like him, using the word 'monsters', Greta explains her vocation and stresses that she needs Varney's help to solve the mystery of the murdering monks. His reaction points to the subtle shift which continues as the novel's plot nears the end: 'It was nonsense, of course; nobody needed Varney any more than they needed a bout of influenza […] but he had to admit it felt pleasant hearing the lie'.[35] In such shifts, Varney is given the courage to fight the repetitive vicious circle in which his life's plotlines seemed to be stuck. Later, by first hypnotising one of the monks, then helping his friends at the climax of the story, carrying a weak and wounded Ruthven and ending up saving the day, he becomes the hero and is described as looking 'more present in the world' as if this new function as hero rather than villain was giving him more tangibility.[36] The last few pages end on a celebration of their victory where Varney toasts to his friends, 'apparently tasting the word like an unfamiliar delicacy',[37] while the epilogue hints at a potential romantic relationship budding between him and Greta (which is realised in a later volume of the series). By changing Varney's narrative function, Shaw appears to try to redeem the pathetic character and give him a new life, after the many he has already lived. In effect, the neo-Victorian Sir Francis Varney is given a way out from remaining a victim of his own fate, caught in a cycle of crimes and death in the penny blood, and he develops into a typical contemporary hero through a story arc based on a narrative of redemption and of finding a community.

While Sir Francis Varney's appearances in neo-Victorian narratives have also recently begun to multiply in non-mainstream formats,[38] though not in a way that is as significant as in Vivian Shaw's novels, other protagonists of the 1840s best-sellers are barely beginning to enter circulation in recent fiction. G. W. M. Reynolds's main characters in *The Mysteries of London*, despite this penny dreadful's tremendous success at the time of its publication, do not seem to circulate as easily as Sweeney Todd or Varney for instance. Still, the *Mysteries*' famous villain Anthony Tidkins, or the Resurrection Man, does feature in a recent collection entitled *DeadSteam: A Chilling Collection of Dreadpunk Tales of the Dark and Supernatural* (2018), in a short story entitled 'Burke Street Station' by Bryce Raffle. This appearance, along with the re-surfacing of Todd and of Varney, seems to fit within Benjamin Poore's argument about Victorian villains 'crossing over from their allotted narratives'[39] since the villains are the *only* characters who cross over from their narratives and who succeed in contributing to the circulation of their source text. In this case, however, Anthony Tidkin's neo-Victorian version loses some of its depth as a character as it takes on a different function from its original iteration, but helps to raise important questions about what actually constitutes a successful circulation.

In 'Burke Street Station', the story is set in a very foggy London, in a historical setting clearly signalled as nineteenth century. The title of the short story itself is a hint to William Burke who, together with William Hare, acted as grave-robbers and so-called resurrectionists to provide corpses to anatomist Robert Knox for his lectures. To meet demand with sufficient supply, they committed a series of at least sixteen homicides in Edinburgh in 1828. Eventually, the Burke and Hare murders and their larger context led to the passing of the Anatomy Act in 1832. Consequently, the title of the short story already foreshadows issues of bodysnatching, murder and circulation of bodies – it is therefore only fitting that the story should feature the famous penny blood villain known as the Resurrection Man, though characters never actually meet him. Hints at the nineteenth century multiply in the setting of the story: the underground station is lit by oil lamps, the stray page of a newspaper picked up by a character features an engraving rather than a photograph, two of the characters of the story are young toshers who make a living scavenging in sewer tunnels and the river mud, other boys are said to work at a blacking factory, and the first of the story's three focalizers is an illiterate young man. There is, however, no indication whether Victoria is the reigning monarch in this setting, and an offhand comment about how 'Prince Charles' was brought 'back from the brink of death' remains unexplained.[40] This helps set the scene in a fantasy alternative to Victorian Britain, which in actual fact did not include any Prince Charles.[41] This setting is also interspersed with retro-futuristic elements typical of the steampunk genre: one of the toshers wears fish-eyed goggles with 'bug-eyed lenses, making his every blink look like the shutter of a camera' and which have day and night settings[42]; the London Underground is steam-powered but has automatic, driverless trains and there is air travel, under the name of aether. The service station also has a room 'filled end to end with copper pipes, valves, and wheels' as well as iron pipes with 'steam hiss[ing] out' and a storage space 'cluttered with stacks of dusty boxes and shelves lined with mildewing books', which provides a traditional steampunk décor.[43]

Anthony Tidkins appears in the story as early as the second paragraph, but his presence throughout is never more than mentions by other characters, as if he were haunting the story. Readers first encounter him in the form of an engraving in a 'Wanted' notice found on a discarded newspaper page picked up by the poverty-stricken, illiterate Theodore, whose inner focalisation constitutes the first part of the story, and he identifies Tidkins 'even without a skill for reading'.[44] In Raffle's storyworld, Tidkins is the head of the Resurrectionists, who are scientists 'named [...] after the sack-em-up men who provided the anatomists with subjects for their scientific endeavours'; these scientists are presented by an admiring Theodore as having 'revolutioni[sed] air travel' and 'devised the engines for the [automatic trains of the] London Underground'.[45] But the Resurrectionists also are murderers, who operate with surgical precision on their victims' corpses as they experiment to bring them back to life as zombies. In this storyworld, so-called resurrection men aim to work literally as they experiment to find a way to cure death, murdering for science and, paradoxically, for life. The leader of the group 'Anthony Tidkins himself promised to cure death'[46] – which displays the gap between lower classes, to whom this might seem hopeful, and higher classes, who consider Tidkins a criminal who must be stopped if the 'Wanted' notice is to be believed.

The story includes more intertextual hints – the investigating duo of Detective Inspector Taggert and Sir Roderick Steen echoes and reproduces the dynamics between Scotland Yard detectives and Sherlock Holmes; the Resurrectionist group includes a certain Mr Hyde, too, apparently less clinical in his ways – but they are not exploited further, and it is the dead body and its potential return that maintain a crucial space in the plot. When the two young boys, Thomas and Fish, follow the trail of blood into the dark and foggy underground tunnels to investigate, Thomas is attacked and dragged away by 'something' that turns out to be responsible for the first murder as well as Thomas's:

> Lips lined with blood, flesh falling away from his cheeks, eyes white with cataracts, a dead man stared back at him. Bones exposed through gaping holes in his rotting flesh, skin blackened and necrotic like the corpse in the station, the man who stood before him looked like he'd dragged himself out of a grave. [...] He reached down, picked out another piece of red, raw meat, and shoved it in his rotting jaws.[47]

The 'dead man', only referred to from then on as 'deader' or 'corpse' and dehumanised through the alternating use of the pronouns 'he' and 'it', is found feasting on Thomas's body in an extremely gruesome depiction of cannibalism. This description of the living dead provides another link to bodysnatching as he 'looked like he'd dragged himself out of a grave': not only is it a corpse that is out of its grave, but it is even a reanimated corpse, who seems to have left its grave of its own accord. DI Taggert and Sir Roderick Steen conclude at the end of the story that the living corpse was in fact the result of the Resurrectionists' experiments, as Steen asks Taggert: 'Isn't that exactly the sort of scientific pursuit our own villain, Anthony Tidkins, might attempt?'[48] – confirming the status of Tidkins as villain and the unwelcome nature of his experiments, through this rhetorical question.

The original political potential of the character of Anthony Tidkins is not picked up or furthered in this neo-Victorian Tidkins-story. In accordance with the political dimension of Reynolds's original penny blood, the Resurrectionists' work in 'Burke Street Station' could have represented the lower class taking a form of action that allows them to become a threat to the established social hierarchy, literally 'eating the rich' by unleashing cannibalistic zombies as a way to overturn the power balance if the victims had been from higher classes. But what represented hope for poor illiterate

Theodore instead provokes his demise, as both victims of the resuscitated corpse are lower-class characters. This cruel irony is reinforced by the fact that the story finishes with the only non-lower class focalizer, DI Taggert, and that Sir Roderick Steen, incidentally the only character with a title, is the one who unequivocally draws the conclusion of Tidkins's guilt and thus controls the narrative. In this, 'Burke Street Station' misses – or chooses not to draw on – the opportunity to live up to Reynolds's character's originally openly political criticism of the class system and of capitalism. Here, the higher classes emerge unscathed and are under no real threat, while the lower-class cannibalises itself. The radical villain who originally served to denounce social determinism and staunchly criticise the establishment is simplified as Tidkins is revealed to be the mastermind behind experiments branded an abomination while remaining absent, the bogeyman of the story. However, if Raffle's neo-Victorian reimagining of the Resurrection Man does not adopt or further a political agenda like *The Mysteries of London* explicitly did, it still contributes productively to the diachronic circulation of penny dreadfuls: in a way, the very fact that Tidkins becomes shorthand for nineteenth-century urban criminal proves the status shift of the penny dreadfuls as they circulate through neo-Victorian culture, in the process of becoming an established cultural reference.

Becoming a Cultural Reference

At the apex of this diachronic circulation, this chapter demonstrates the fact that the penny dreadful genre and its codes can actually be identified in recent neo-Victorian fiction works and become relied upon as a cultural reference, a literary landmark that is gradually taking the place it was long denied. Connecting to Nadine Böhm-Schnitker and Susanne Gruss's argument that 'as a cultural practice, (neo-Victorian) adaptations fashion our cultural memory, create cultural value in confirming the status of canonised works, document the "hereditary" transmissions of cultural content',[49] the growing frequency of penny blood or penny dreadful references in neo-Victorian narratives points towards efforts to question the canon and reconsider cultural value in establishing a new feature, or as Sonia Solicari formulates it, a new 'path of inspiration' that comes to coincide with others at the crossroads which produce Victoriana.[50] Neo-Victoriana establishing this penny blood path of inspiration allows for new crossroads with other established paths and therefore gives rise to new potential ways of engaging critically with the Victorian past, considering that the tradition of penny bloods and penny dreadfuls is markedly associated with lower-class culture and a different form of literature and storytelling than the literary canon. The development of this diachronic circulation therefore creates opportunities for neo-Victorian fiction to experiment with new ways to speak about the past, in more or less mainstream formats and with a focus on the popular.

In her foreword to the *DeadSteam* collection, which includes 'Burke Street Station', Leanna Renee Hieber explains that the anthology contributes to the Dreadpunk subgenre, a term coined by Derek Tatum in 2015 in an attempt to create a new category bringing together modern expressions of the Victorian Gothic and the Steampunk genres. In essence, 'Dreadpunk's steam is dread; the narrative is powered by a slow-mounting fear of what's happening, what's perceived and what may happen next'; and the 'punk' component is described as seeking to challenge power structures and question the 'divisive and exclusionary natures of imbalanced power dynamics'.[51] Hieber claims that Dreadpunk has its 'roots in the Gothic and "Penny Dreadful" literary tradition'[52]; and while this recently coined category may still struggle to distinguish itself from other existing Gothic subgenres, the use of penny dreadfuls as a reference point marks the shift in cultural value that is slowly being operated. The cheap publications thus acquire a status within the 'hereditary transmissions of cultural content'[53] that form part of the cultural value of neo-Victorianism.

In addition to becoming an established (and explicitly recognised) inspiration for many neo-Victorian works, some of the codes of the penny bloods and penny dreadfuls' literary tradition are being appropriated and adapted, too, to become part of a broader Victoriana in works that do not mention them directly. This is the case in my final example, Laura Carlin's *The Wicked Cometh* (2018). Contrary to the works previously discussed, this novel does not contain any direct mention of penny bloods or penny dreadfuls; neither do they play a part in its plot.[54] Even the few potential indirect references seem to hint at historical context more than at penny publications per se. When, early on, the orphaned protagonist Hester tells her adoptive aunt that she has been 'reading the discarded newspapers at the market', this remark is not met by any judgement on the type of reading material or the way it was acquired considering that they live in extreme poverty, and Hester's aunt simply encourages her to keep talking.[55] This scene hints at some of the consumption practices to which lower-class readers of the time had recourse, since they were often compelled to procure reading material in ways far more creative (and appropriate to their everyday life) than by entering the marketplace as customers. It evokes Mayhew's accounts of costermongers wrapping the products they sold in old sheets of newspapers or periodicals, thus recycling the reading material into something with a practical use, which some customers would then turn back into reading material.[56] This full circle is exactly what Carlin's protagonist participates in – but though the quoted passage refers to potential consumption practices of the early nineteenth-century lower-class readership that are relevant in the penny blood context, it cannot be considered a reference to penny bloods given the chronological setting of the novel.

From its beginning, the story is explicitly set in 1831. The fact that there are no direct references to penny bloods therefore makes perfect sense as such occurrences would be anachronistic, bearing in mind that the penny blood market mostly developed consistently from the time of Charles Dickens's serialised publication of the *Pickwick Papers* in 1836 onwards. The *Wicked Cometh* storyline, in other words, takes place before this cheap literature boom. However, Carlin's novel opens with a fictional *Morning Herald* newspaper cutting (dated Tuesday, 13 September 1831) bearing the mention 'Price One Penny' now famously associated with penny fiction instalments. The London *Morning Herald* did in fact exist at the time – founded in 1780, it ran until 1869 – and the fictional cut-out included in *The Wicked Cometh* uses a virtually identical typeface for its title as the historical *Morning Herald*. But the price listed on Laura Carlin's version of the paper does not correspond to the price of this newspaper at the time, as archival research shows (see Figure 4.1). The front page of the issue of *The Morning Herald* dated 13 September 1831, i.e. of the same date as its fictional counterpart, shows the price as seven pence rather than one penny. Issues published months or even years before and after this precise number confirm that this is not a particular case or a differently priced issue, as the price of seven pence for a daily number is found consistently. This fact, along with the use of the same font for the name of the newspaper, indicates that Carlin was indeed familiar with the source publication but purposefully chose to list a different price on her fictional front page.

Since the price that the author chose for her fictional newspaper clearly departs from its historical counterpart, I can only read 'Price One Penny' as a resolute hint to penny blood publications. It is, after all, what constitutes part of the name they inherited. Moreover, this precise formulation of the price in this very physical space on the page (top right-hand corner, aligned with the date) and along with its specific capitalisation used to be a feature on the front page of instalments issued by the most prolific publishers of penny bloods, from Lloyd to Reynolds. Though it was used by other publications, too, this feature soon became typical of penny blood serialisations, while other types of penny

Figure 4.1 Front page of issue n°15,933 of *The Morning Herald*, dated Tuesday, 13 September 1831.

publications employed different formulations: Charles Knight's *Penny Magazine* for instance, created in 1832 for the SDUK, did not list a price on individual instalments at all – its title was considered enough. 'Price One Penny' has therefore become one of the identifying criteria of, and almost shorthand for, penny bloods.[57] Carlin's fictional newspaper page, however, does not feature a work of fiction to remind us of penny bloods, but a news story. This further explains why the author did not choose the name of an actual periodical priced one penny: as these were not officially newspapers, they were not allowed to run news items, or they would have been liable to paying the newspaper tax. Periodicals running penny bloods often ran news stories under the cover of fiction, deleting dates or key names to circumvent this tax. Since a clear and factual news story was necessary for the purposes of Carlin's novel's opening, the name of an actual newspaper of the time was thus far more relevant there. Yet by choosing to feature this particular phrase, which in fact only took on its cultural relevance a few years after 1831, Carlin uses her creative license to bring a certain form of reading material closer to her poverty-stricken protagonist and the marketplace she frequents – the seven-pence *Morning Herald* indeed belonged to other spheres – while allowing the plot device necessary to open the story. While the direct reference to penny bloods is lost, as it is not relevant to the plot, the phrase 'Price One Penny' takes on a form of independence from its original publication context, acting as the representation of a certain place in society and thus becoming a code for popular literature of the nineteenth century.

Contemporary resonances such as the ones traced in this last chapter prove that penny dreadfuls continue to circulate diachronically in several ways, preserving the dynamism of the original genre while evolving through the landscape of contemporary entertainment. When combining this open-ended diachronic circulation and its multiplying references with the other forms of circulation traced in the penny dreadfuls' history and throughout this book, a pattern begins to emerge, resembling a fractal shape – that is to say, a seemingly never-ending, simple yet complex, geometric figure with a degree of self-similarity. Fractal patterns combine irregularity and iteration, and pervade the natural world, often unnoticed. But once the eye becomes trained to recognise them, their presence becomes obvious, and overwhelming in its scale. I argue that the case of the penny dreadful genre forms a fractal shape that is built with circulation patterns, which once recognised, seem to multiply ceaselessly. Different yet similar, these patterns are found in all the dimensions of the penny dreadful phenomenon and problematize the penny dreadfuls' relationship with their contemporary society, as they interact with existing shapes and appropriate a variety of elements while ensuring constant movement. Exploiting more figurative meanings of the term 'circulation', as a movement within an established system (in this case, within the network of late-eighteenth-century and early-nineteenth-century popular literature and culture), allowed penny dreadfuls to define their own contours by placing themselves at the intersection of several trends that constituted the 'popular', such as oral storytelling, sensationalism and the Gothic, and appropriating them at will. Their complex nature, in that they cannot be located within one precise genre and thus develop their own, is also their strength, as their malleability and fluidity created productive spaces to constantly reinvent themselves amidst debates over the hegemonic discourse of what should and should not be read. As the readership that was new to literacy experimented and developed its own tastes, penny dreadfuls could thus keep mutating thanks to this circulation, ensuring their continued popularity, and these tensions in the literary marketplace mirror contemporary changes on a social, cultural and political level. The fractal keeps expanding, as its nature requires, and the uncovering of the overarching patterns of circulation of penny dreadfuls across popular culture and beyond their own century gradually brings out a questioning of the distribution of social power, teaching us about the place – and the power – of class in the development of popular culture and of literature.

All in all, through the lens of the concept of circulation which pervades the penny dreadfuls' history and content, this study shows the importance of the phenomenon to better understand broader notions of popular culture and to keep deconstructing such binaries as 'high' and 'low' culture. The fact that penny dreadfuls were so subversive and unconfined is tied to their significant cultural place at the nexus between social change, technological developments, political tensions, new consumption patterns and the redefinition of literature. Consequently, they also raise the broader issue of the necessity to analyse literature not only as content but as an object published within a certain format and set of rules; or in other words, about the entanglement of literature with material culture. Ultimately, a transversal approach through the concept of circulation allows for scholarship that does not consider penny dreadfuls as *either* a sociocultural curiosity *or* as literature – but that rather asks how the dimensions intersect, and what this produced.

Circulation interweaves numerous aspects of popular culture and of the publishing phenomenon that is the penny dreadful in particular. It can connect the material and the literary, thematise a wide spectrum of political, social and cultural content, and bring into contact the behaviour of the phenomenon in the marketplace, its reception (whether positive or negative), and its legacy. As a result, the concept renders possible a reappraisal of the penny dreadfuls' role in their contemporary society as well as of their impact. The fact that the influence of these publications on other genres can be traced over centuries, all the way to recent neo-Victorian popular narratives, shows beyond doubt that the fractal of circulation patterns of penny dreadfuls keeps expanding.

Notes

1. See Weltman 2009; Haugtvedt 2016; Weltman 2020; Labrande 2020.
2. See Llewellyn 2008; Heilmann and Llewellyn 2010; Mitchell 2010; Cox 2012; Böhm-Schnitker and Gruss 2014.
3. See Poore 2017; Wells-Lassagne and Voigts 2021; Grossman and Scheibel 2023.
4. See Poore and Jones 2009; Grossman and Scheibel 2023; Becker 2023.
5. Parry, *Way of All Flesh*, 168.
6. Ibid.
7. Ibid., 11.
8. Thomson, *Beloved Poison*, 31.
9. Ibid.
10. Ibid., 32.
11. Ibid., 180.
12. Ibid., 173.
13. Burz-Labrande, '"Useful Knowledge" versus "Wastes of Print"', 127–130.
14. Thomson, *Beloved Poison*, 110, 180, 180, 384.
15. Ibid., 183.
16. Ibid., 173–174.
17. Mayhew and Mayhew, *Greatest Plague of Life*, 172, 112, emphasis original.
18. For more about the Mayhew brothers' character of Betsy, see James 1982.
19. Thomson, *Beloved Poison*, 174.
20. While Elaine Showalter's research in *The Female Malady: Women, Madness and English Culture, 1830–1980* (1987) shows that the larger proportion of people in asylums after the 1850s were women (p. 52), Valerie Pedlar stresses that these statistics do not always show a weighty difference and must be qualified: 'the figures that Showalter quotes show that even as late as 1871, the census returns record a ratio of 1,182 female lunatics for every 1,000 male lunatics. These figures concerned lunatics who were confined in various public institutions, the county asylums, licensed houses, workhouses, and in single care. Men still predominated in private madhouses, asylums for the criminally insane, military hospitals and idiot schools' (p. 15).
21. Shaw, *Strange Practice*, 3–4.
22. Ibid., 6.
23. Oliphant, 'Byways of Literature', 202.
24. Shaw, *Strange Practice*, 96.
25. Ibid., 203.
26. See Weltman 2009; Poore and Jones 2009; Haugtvedt 2016; Weltman 2020; Labrande 2020; Nesvet 2024.
27. Shaw, *Strange Practice*, 85.
28. See Frayling 1992; Holstein 2010: Collins Jenkins 2010.
29. Poore, 'Villain-Effect', 1.
30. Shaw, *Strange Practice*, 254.
31. Ibid., 5.
32. Ibid., 203.
33. Rymer, *Varney, the Vampire*, 37.
34. Shaw, *Strange Practice*, 125–126.
35. Ibid., 206.
36. Ibid., 345.

37 Ibid.
38 In 2011, a Kickstarter campaign was launched to fund a *Varney the Vampire* comic book series, created by Scott Massino and Marcio Takara. The first two numbers were produced, but the project was put on hold until another funding campaign in 2014, which did not reach its goal.

    In 2016, a one-season web series based on the penny blood entitled *Varney the Vampire or the Feast of Blood* was released (with 29 episodes – see https://www.imdb.com/title/tt3510440/).

    In 2021, Varney featured in the fourth season of Netflix's dark fantasy animated television series *Castlevania*, in which he turns out to be the Grim Reaper, an eternal being who – ironically – seeks to bring Dracula back from the dead.
39 Poore, 'Villain-Effect', 1.
40 Raffle, 'Burke Street Station', 12.
41 Queen Victoria did not have any children named Charles, and she is not known to have suffered any miscarriage or stillbirths, either – which rules her out as the monarch in this short story.
42 Ibid., 17.
43 Ibid., 29, 34, 30.
44 Ibid., 12.
45 Ibid.
46 Ibid.
47 Ibid., 23, 31.
48 Ibid., 38.
49 Böhm-Schnitker and Gruss, 'Fashioning the Neo-Victorian', 7.
50 Solicari, 'Is This Neo-Victorian?', 182.
51 Hieber, 'Foreword', viii, viii.
52 Ibid., viii.
53 Böhm-Schnitker and Gruss, 'Fashioning the Neo-Victorian', 7.
54 The novel only includes a (single) mention of penny gaffs (p. 17), the theatres that formed part of the street culture to which the penny bloods were born (see Jacobs 2015).
55 Carlin, *The Wicked Cometh*, 10.
56 Mayhew, *London Labour*, 1: 28 and 2: 114.
57 In scholarship, too, as shown by Marie Léger-St-Jean's choice to use the phrase as the title of her database of penny fiction: http://www.priceonepenny.info/.

BIBLIOGRAPHY

Abraham, Adam. 'Dickens, "Dickensian," and the Pseudo-Dickens Industry'. *SEL Studies in English Literature 1500-1900* 57, no. 4 (1 December 2017): 751–770. https://doi.org/10.1353/sel.2017.0033.
Altick, Richard D. *The English Common Reader: A Social History of the Mass Reading Public, 1800–1900*. 2nd ed. Columbus: Ohio State University Press, 1998.
Arnold, Matthew. *Culture and Anarchy*. Edited by Jane Garnett. Oxford; New York: Oxford University Press, 2006.
Banks, J. A. 'The Contagion of Numbers'. In *The Victorian City: Images and Realities*, edited by Harold James Dyos and Michael Wolff, 105–123. London: Routledge, 1999.
Basdeo, Stephen. 'The Politics of Victorian England's "Vicious Republican": G. W. M. Reynolds (1814–79)'. Reynolds's News and Miscellany, 13 February 2019. http://reynolds-news.com/2019/02/13/the-politics-of-victorian-englands-vicious-republican-g-w-m-reynolds-1814-79-stephen-basdeo/.
Batty, Michael, Elena Besussi, and Nancy Chin. 'Traffic, Urban Growth and Suburban Sprawl'. *UCL Centre for Advanced Spatial Analysis Working Papers Series*, no. 70 (10 November 2003).
Bearne, Eve. 'Multimodality, Literacy and Texts: Developing a Discourse'. *Journal of Early Childhood Literacy* 9, no. 2 (1 August 2009): 156–187. https://doi.org/10.1177/1468798409105585.
Becker, Christine. 'The Adaptive Marketing of Penny Dreadful: Listening to The Dreadfuls'. In *Penny Dreadful and Adaptation: Reanimating and Transforming the Monster*, edited by Julie Grossman and Will Scheibel, 31–47. Cham: Springer International Publishing, 2023.
Bleiler, E. F. '"Introduction" to the Dover Edition'. In *Varney, the Vampire: Or, The Feast of Blood*, edited by Curt Herr, 784–790. Crestline: Zittaw Press, 2008.
Bloom, Harold. *The Anxiety of Influence: A Theory of Poetry*. 2nd ed. New York: Oxford University Press, 1997.
Böhm-Schnitker, Nadine, and Susanne Gruss. 'Introduction: Fashioning the Neo-Victorian – Neo-Victorian Fashions'. In *Neo-Victorian Literature and Culture: Immersions and Revisitations*, edited by Nadine Böhm-Schnitker and Susanne Gruss, 1–20. New York; Abingdon: Routledge, 2014.
Bolton, Reginald Pelham. 'The Cockney and His Dialect'. *The Journal of American Folklore* 8, no. 30 (September 1895): 222–229.
Bootle Times. 'Old Boys' Periodicals'. 30 June 1916.
Bos [Thomas Peckett Prest]. *Nickelas Nickelbery*. London: E. Lloyd, Broad Street, Bloomsbury, 1838.

———. *The Sketch-Book by 'Bos,' Containing a Great Number of Highly Interesting and Original Tales, Sketches, &c. &c. Embellished with Seventeen Elegant Engravings*. London: Printed and published by E. Lloyd, 1837.

Botting, Fred. *Gothic*. The New Critical Idiom. London; New York: Routledge, 1996.

Bowley, A. L. *Wages in the United Kingdom in the Nineteenth Century*. Cambridge University Press, 1900. http://archive.org/details/wagesinunitedkin00bowl.

Brake, Laurel. 'Markets, Genres, Iterations'. In *The Routledge Handbook to Nineteenth-Century British Periodicals and Newspapers*, edited by Andrew King, Alexis Easley, and John Morton, 237–248. London: Routledge, 2016.

Burz-Labrande, Manon. '"Embalmed Pestilence", "Intoxicating Poisons": Rhetoric of Contamination, Contagion, and the Gothic Marginalisation of Penny Dreadfuls by Their Contemporary Critics'. In *Penny Dreadfuls and the Gothic: Investigations of Pernicious Tales of Terror*, edited by Nicole C. Dittmer and Sophie Raine, 91–113. Cardiff: University of Wales Press, 2023.

———. '"Useful Knowledge" versus "Wastes of Print": Working-Class Education and Edward Lloyd'. *Victorian Popular Fictions* 3, no. 1 (Spring 2021): 123–139. https://doi.org/10.46911/QODX5600.

Burz-Labrande, Manon, and Marie Léger-St-Jean. '"Lost, as It Were, from amidst the Assemblage of My Literary Productions": Authorial Agency from Scissors-and-Paste to Remix in Reynolds's Translations'. In *G.W.M. Reynolds Reimagined: Studies in Authorship, Radicalism, and Genre, 1830–1870*, edited by Jennifer Conary and Mary L. Shannon, 52–81. New York: Routledge, 2023.

Carlin, Laura. *The Wicked Cometh*. London: Hodder and Stoughton, 2018.

Carlisle, Janice. 'Popular and Mass-Market Fiction'. In *A Companion to the English Novel*, edited by Stephen Arata, Madigan Haley, J. Paul Hunter, and Jennifer Wicke, 132–143. Chichester: John Wiley & Sons, Ltd, 2015.

'Castlevania'. Netflix, 2017–2021.

Chapman, Raymond. *Forms of Speech in Victorian Fiction*. London and New York: Longman, 1994.

Chavez, Julia McCord. 'The Gothic Heart of Victorian Serial Fiction'. *Studies in English Literature, 1500-1900* 50, no. 4 (2010): 791–810.

Chesterton, G. K. 'A Defence of Penny Dreadfuls'. *The Speaker* 3, no. 75 (16 March 1901): 648–649.

Cleave's London Satirist and Gazette of Variety. 'Nickelas Nickelbery'. 31 March 1838.

Clery, E. J. 'The Genesis of "Gothic" Fiction'. In *The Cambridge Companion to Gothic Fiction*, edited by Jerrold E. Hogle, 21–39. Cambridge: Cambridge University Press, 2002.

Cockton, Henry. *The Life and Adventures of Valentine Vox, the Ventriloquist*. London: W. Nicholson & sons, Limited, n.d.

Cohen, Monica F. *Pirating Fictions: Ownership and Creativity in Nineteenth-Century Popular Culture*. Charlottesville: University of Virginia Press, 2017.

———. 'Unintended Authors: Piracy, Plagiarism and Property in Victorian Popular Culture'. *Victorian Popular Fictions Journal* 3, no. 2 (2021): 1–20. https://doi.org/10.46911/AMTW8511.

Colclough, Stephen. *Consuming Texts: Readers and Reading Communities, 1695–1870*. New York: Palgrave Macmillan, 2007.

Collins, Wilkie. 'The Unknown Public'. *Household Words* 18 (1858): 217–222.

Collins Jenkins, Mark. *Vampire Forensics: Uncovering the Origins of an Enduring Legend*. Washington: National Geographic, 2010.

Conary, Jennifer, and Mary L. Shannon, eds. *G.W.M. Reynolds Reimagined: Studies in Authorship, Radicalism, and Genre, 1830–1870*. New York: Routledge, 2023.

Cox, Alfred. *Among the Doctors*. London: C. Johnson, 1950.

Cox, Jessica. 'Neo-Victorianism'. Oxford Bibliographies. Oxford University Press, 24 April 2012. https://doi.org/10.1093/obo/9780199799558-0083.

Cunningham, Hugh. *Leisure in the Industrial Revolution: C. 1780–c. 1880*. London: Routledge, 1980. https://doi.org/10.4324/9781315637679.

Dalziel, Margaret. *Popular Fiction 100 Years Ago: An Unexplored Tract of Literary History*. London: Cohen & West, 1957.

Deacon, Roger. 'Moral Orthopedics: A Foucauldian Account of Schooling as Discipline'. *Telos: Critical Theory of the Contemporary* Spring 2005, no. 130 (2005): 84–102.

Deazley, Ronan. 'Commentary on Copyright Amendment Act 1842'. Primary Sources on Copyright (1450–1900), eds L. Bently & M. Kretschmer, 2008. https://www.copyrighthistory.org/cam/tools/request/showRecord.php?id=commentary_uk_1842.

Delafield, Catherine. *Serialization and the Victorian Novel in Mid-Victorian Magazines*. Farnham: Ashgate, 2015.

Diamond, Michael. *Victorian Sensation, or, The Spectacular, the Shocking, and the Scandalous in Nineteenth-Century Britain*. London: Anthem Press, 2004.

Dickens, Charles. *Nicholas Nickleby*. Edited by Mark Ford. Penguin Classics. London; New York: Penguin Books, 1999.

Dittmer, Nicole C., and Sophie Raine, eds. *Penny Dreadfuls and the Gothic: Investigations of Pernicious Tales of Terror*. Cardiff: University of Wales Press, 2023.

Dixon, William Hepworth. 'The Literature of the Lower Orders. Batch the First'. *Daily News* 440 (26 October 1847): 3.

Downes, Daragh, and Trish Ferguson, eds. *Victorian Fiction beyond the Canon*. London: Palgrave Macmillan, 2016.

Dunae, Patrick A. 'Penny Dreadfuls: Late Nineteenth-Century Boys' Literature and Crime'. *Victorian Studies* 22, no. 2 (Winter 1979): 133–150.

Eco, Umberto. 'Interpreting Serials'. *The Limits of Interpretation*, 83–100. Bloomington: Indiana University Press, 1994.

Edwards, P. D. *Some Mid-Victorian Thrillers: The Sensation Novel, Its Friends and Its Foes*. St Lucia: University of Queensland Press, 1971.

Flanders, Judith. *The Invention of Murder*. London: HarperPress, 2011.

Foucault, Michel. *Discipline and Punish: The Birth of the Prison*. Harmondsworth: Peregrine, 1975.

———. 'Of Other Spaces'. Translated by Jay Miskowiec. *Diacritics* 16, no. 1 (1986): 22–27. https://doi.org/10.2307/464648.

———. 'The Order of Discourse'. In *Modern and Postmodern Rhetoric*, edited by Patricia Bizzell and Bruce Herzberg, 1460–1470. Boston: Bedford, 2011.

Frayling, Christopher. *Vampyres: Lord Byron to Count Dracula*. London; Boston: Faber and Faber, 1992.

Frohn, Celine. 'A Ventriloquist and a Highwayman Walk into an Inn… Early Penny Bloods and the Politics of Humour in Valentine Vaux and Sixteen-String Jack'. In *Penny Dreadfuls and the Gothic: Investigations of Pernicious Tales of Terror*, edited by Nicole C. Dittmer and Sophie Raine, 161–179. Cardiff: University of Wales Press, 2023.

'G.W.M. Reynolds'. *The Bookseller* 240 (3 July 1879): 600–601.

Garrett, Peter K. *Gothic Reflections: Narrative Force in Nineteenth-Century Fiction*. Ithaca: Cornell University Press, 2003.

Gasperini, Anna. *Nineteenth Century Popular Fiction, Medicine and Anatomy: The Victorian Penny Blood and the 1832 Anatomy Act*. New York: Palgrave Macmillan, 2019.
Geddes, Patrick. *Cities in Evolution*. New York: Harper & Row, 1915.
Goldblatt, David. *Art and Ventriloquism*. London: Routledge, 2006.
Greenwood, James. 'A Short Way to Newgate'. In *The Wilds of London*, 158–172. London: Chatto and Windus, 1874.
Grossman, Julie, and Will Scheibel, eds. *Penny Dreadful and Adaptation: Reanimating and Transforming the Monster*. Cham, Switzerland: Palgrave Macmillan, 2023.
Halliday, M. A. K. *Language as a Social Semiotic: The Social Interpretation of Language and Meaning*. London: Edward Arnold, 1978.
Harris, R. W. *England in the 18th Century: A Balanced Constitution and New Horizons*. London: Blanford Press, 1963.
Haugtvedt, Erica. 'Sweeney Todd as Victorian Transmedial Storyworld'. *Victorian Periodicals Review* 49, no. 3 (2016): 443–460.
Hayward, Jennifer. *Consuming Pleasures: Active Audiences and Serial Fictions from Dickens to Soap Opera*. Lexington: University Press of Kentucky, 1997.
Haywood, Ian. 'George W.M. Reynolds and "The Trafalgar Square Revolution": Radicalism, the Carnivalesque and Popular Culture in Mid-Victorian England'. *Journal of Victorian Culture* 7, no. 1 (1 January 2002): 23–59. https://doi.org/10.3366/jvc.2002.7.1.23.
———. *The Revolution in Popular Literature: Print, Politics and the People, 1790–1860*. Cambridge: Cambridge University Press, 2003.
Heilmann, Ann, and Mark Llewellyn. *Neo-Victorianism: The Victorians in the Twenty-First Century, 1999–2009*. Basingstoke; New York: Palgrave Macmillan, 2010.
Hieber, Leanna Renee. 'Foreword'. In *Deadsteam: A Chilling Collection of Dreadpunk Tales of the Dark and Supernatural*, edited by Bryce Raffle, vii–x. Grimmer & Grimmer Books, 2018.
Hoggart, Paul. 'Travesties of Dickens'. *Essays and Studies* 40 (1987): 32–44.
Hogle, Jerrold E. 'Introduction: The Gothic in Western Culture'. In *The Cambridge Companion to Gothic Fiction*, edited by Jerrold E. Hogle, 1–20. Cambridge: Cambridge University Press, 2002.
Hollingsworth, Keith. *The Newgate Novel, 1830–1847*. Detroit: Wayne State UP, 1963.
Holstein, Eric. 'Les trois romans fondateurs'. *Bifrost, la revue des mondes imaginaires* 60, no. Sang pour sang: Le réveil des vampires (2010): 126–130.
Hughes, Linda K., and Michael Lund. *The Victorian Serial*. Charlottesville and London: University Press of Virginia, 1991.
Humpherys, Anne. 'Generic Strands and Urban Twists: The Victorian Mysteries Novel'. *Victorian Studies* 34, no. 4 (Summer 1991): 455–472.
———. 'G. W. M. Reynolds, Popular Literature and Popular Politics'. *Victorian Periodicals Review* 16 (1983): 79–89.
———. 'Popular Narrative and Political Discourse in Reynolds's Weekly Newspaper'. In *Investigating Victorian Journalism*, edited by Laurel Brake, Aled Jones, and Lionel Madden, 33–47. New York: St Martin's, 1990.
———. 'The Geometry of the Modern City: G. W. M. Reynolds and "The Mysteries of London"'. *Browning Institute Studies* 11 (1983): 69–80.
Humpherys, Anne, and Louis James, eds. *G.W.M. Reynolds: Nineteenth-Century Fiction, Politics, and the Press*. London: Routledge, 2008.

Hutcheon, Linda. *A Theory of Adaptation*. 2nd edition. New York; Abingdon: Routledge, 2006.

Jacobs, Edward. 'Disvaluing the Popular: London Street Culture, "Industrial Literacy", and the Emergence of Mass Culture in Victorian England'. In *Victorian Urban Settings: Essays on the Nineteenth-Century City and Its Contexts*, edited by Debra N. Mancoff and D. J. Trela, 89–113. New York: Routledge, 2015.

James, Elizabeth, and Helen R. Smith, eds. *Penny Dreadfuls and Boys' Adventures: The Barry Ono Collection of Victorian Popular Literature in the British Library*. London: British Library, 1998.

James, Louis. *Fiction for the Working Man 1830–1850: A Study of the Literature Produced for the Working Classes in Early Victorian Urban England*. London: Oxford University Press, 1963.

———. 'The Trouble with Betsy: Periodicals and the Common Reader in Mid-Nineteenth Century England'. In *The Victorian Periodical Press: Samplings and Soundings*, edited by Joanne Shattock and Michael Wolff, 349–366. Leicester: Leicester University Press, 1982.

———. 'The View from Brick Lane: Contrasting Perspectives in Working-Class and Middle-Class Fiction of the Early Victorian Period'. *The Yearbook of English Studies* 11 (1981): 87–101. https://doi.org/10.2307/3506260.

Kaplan, Fred. *Dickens: A Biography*. London: Hodder & Stoughton, 1988.

Kelleter, Frank, ed. *Media of Serial Narrative*. Columbus: Ohio State University Press, 2017.

Kickstarter. 'Varney the Vampire: A Six-Issue Series for Image Comics', 24 February 2014. https://www.kickstarter.com/projects/varneythevampire/varney-the-vampire-a-tale-of-arteries-and-absoluti.

King, Andrew. '"Literature of the Kitchen": Cheap Serial Fiction of the 1840s and 1850s'. In *A Companion to Sensation Fiction*, edited by Pamela K. Gilbert, 38–53. Chichester: Wiley-Blackwell, 2011.

King, Andrew, Alexis Easley, and John Morton. 'Introduction.' In *The Routledge Handbook to Nineteenth-Century British Periodicals and Newspapers*, edited by Andrew King, Alexis Easley and John Morton, 1–13. London: Routledge, 2016.

Knight, Stephen. *G. W. M. Reynolds and His Fiction: The Man Who Outsold Dickens*. London: Routledge, 2018.

Kress, Gunther. *Literacy in the New Media Age*. London: Routledge, 2003.

Kristeva, Julia. *Powers of Horror: An Essay on Abjection*. Translated by Leon S. Roudiez. New York: Columbia University Press, 1982.

Labrande, Manon. '"Attend the Tale of Sweeney Todd": The Transmedial Circulation of a Victorian Narrative'. *Polysèmes. Revue d'études Intertextuelles et Intermédiales*, no. 23 (30 June 2020). https://doi.org/10.4000/polysemes.6781.

Lansdown, Richard. 'The Pickwick Papers: Something Nobler than a Novel?' *Critical Review* 31 (1991): 75–91.

Law, Graham. *Serializing Fiction in the Victorian Press*. Basingstoke; New York: Palgrave, 2000.

Law, Jules. *The Social Life of Fluids: Blood, Milk, and Water in the Victorian Novel*. Ithaca: Cornell University Press, 2010.

Léger-St-Jean, Marie. 'Price One Penny – Cheap Literature 1837–1860'. Accessed 21 September 2025. http://www.priceonepenny.info/index.php.

Lill, Sarah Louise, and Rohan McWilliam, eds. *Edward Lloyd and His World: Popular Fiction, Politics and the Press in Victorian Britain*. New York: Routledge, 2019.

Llewellyn, Mark. 'What Is Neo-Victorian Studies?' *Journal of Neo-Victorian Studies* 1, no. 1 (2008): 164–185.
Lloyd, Edward, ed. *The People's Periodical and Family Library. Vol. 1. No. 1-52. 10 Oct. 1846-2 Oct. 1847*. London: Edward Lloyd, 1846.
Loesberg, Jonathan. 'The Ideology of Narrative Form in Sensation Fiction'. *Representations*, no. 13 (1986): 115–138. https://doi.org/10.2307/2928496.
Loock, Kathleen. 'Introduction: Serial Narratives'. In *Serial Narratives*, edited by Kathleen Loock, 5–9. Kiel: Königshausen & Neumann, 2014.
Marx, Karl. *Capital*. New York: International Publishers, 1967.
———. *Grundrisse: Foundations of the Critique of Political Economy (Rough Draft)*. Marxists Internet Archive, 2015. https://www.marxists.org/archive/marx/works/1857/grundrisse/index.htm.
Maunder, Andrew. 'Mapping the Victorian Sensation Novel: Some Recent and Future Trends'. *Literature Compass* 2, no. 1 (2005). https://doi.org/10.1111/j.1741-4113.2005.00140.x.
Mayer, Ruth. *Serial Fu Manchu: The Chinese Supervillain and the Spread of Yellow Peril Ideology*. Philadelphia: Temple University Press, 2014.
Mayhew, Henry. 'A Balloon View of London'. In *The Criminal Prisons of London, and Scenes of Prison Life*, edited by Henry Mayhew and John Binny, 7–10. Griffin, Bohn, and Company, 1862.
———. 'Labour and the Poor: Letter III'. *Morning Chronicle*, 26 October 1849.
———. *London Labour and the London Poor*. Vol. 1. 4 vols. New York: Dover, 1968.
———. *London Labour and the London Poor*. Vol. 2. 4 vols. New York: Dover, 1968.
———. *London Labour and the London Poor*. Vol. 3. 4 vols. New York: Dover, 1968.
Mayhew, Henry, and Augustus Mayhew. *The Greatest Plague of Life; or, the Adventures of a Lady in Search of a Good Servant*. Philadelphia: Carey and Hart, 1847.
Meteyard, Eliza. 'Cheap Literature'. In *Ragged School Union Magazine*, II:219–222. London: Partridge & Oakey, Paternoster Row, 1849.
Mieszkowski, Sylvia, and Barbara Straumann. 'Force Fields of Serial Narration'. In *Anglistentag 2016 Proceedings*, edited by Ute Berns, 151–160. Trier: WVT Wissenschaftler Verlag, 2017.
Mighall, Robert. *A Geography of Victorian Gothic Fiction: Mapping History's Nightmares*. Oxford: Oxford University Press, 2003.
Milbank, Alison. 'The Victorian Gothic in English Novels and Stories, 1830–1880'. In *The Cambridge Companion to Gothic Fiction*, edited by Jerrold E. Hogle, 145–165. Cambridge: Cambridge University Press, 2002.
Miles, Robert. 'The 1790s: The Effulgence of Gothic'. In *The Cambridge Companion to Gothic Fiction*, edited by Jerrold E. Hogle, 41–62. Cambridge: Cambridge University Press, 2002.
'Mischievous Literature'. *The Bookseller* 126 (1868): 445–449.
Mitchell, Kate. *History and Cultural Memory in Neo-Victorian Fiction*. Basingstoke: Palgrave Macmillan, 2010.
Mittell, Jason. 'Narrative Complexity in Contemporary American Television'. *The Velvet Light Trap* 58, no. 1 (2006): 29–40. https://doi.org/10.1353/vlt.2006.0032.
Nesvet, Rebecca. *James Malcolm Rymer, Penny Fiction, and the Family*. New York: Routledge, 2025.
———. '"Like a Polish'd Razor Keen": Sweeney Todd, Figaro in London, and Transmedia Satire'. *Victorian Popular Fictions Journal* 6, no. 2 (21 December 2024): 29–48. https://doi.org/10.46911/VPAP6681.

Neuburg, Victor E. *Popular Literature, a History and Guide: From the Beginning of Printing to the Year 1897.* London: Woburn Press, 1977.
Oliphant, Margaret. 'The Byways of Literature: Reading for the Million'. *Blackwood's Edinburgh Magazine* 84 (August 1858): 200–216.
Page, Norman. *Speech in the English Novel.* 2nd ed. Basingstoke: Macmillan, 1973.
Parry, Ambrose. *The Way of All Flesh.* Edinburgh: Canongate Books, 2018.
Pedlar, Valerie. *The Most Dreadful Visitation: Male Madness in Victorian Fiction.* Liverpool: Liverpool University Press, 2006.
Penny Dreadful. Showtime Networks, 2014–2016.
Phillips Day, Samuel. *Juvenile Crime, Its Causes, Character, and Cure.* London: J. F. Hope, 1858.
Pitman, Isaac. *A Manual of Phonography; Or, Writing by Sound: A Natural Method of Writing by Signs That Represent the Sounds of Language, and Adapted to the English Language as a Complete System of Phonetic Short Hand.* London: Samuel Bagster and Sons, 1845.
Pittard, Christopher. 'V for Ventriloquism: Powers of Vocal Mimicry in Henry Cockton's The Life and Adventures of Valentine Vox, the Ventriloquist'. *19: Interdisciplinary Studies in the Long Nineteenth Century,* no. 24 (12 May 2017). https://doi.org/10.16995/ntn.778.
Polidori, John. 'The Vampyre'. In *Two Early Vampire Tales: John Polidori's The Vampyre & J. Sheridan Le Fanu's Carmilla,* 5–41. Another Leaf Press, 2012.
Poore, Benjamin. 'The Villain-Effect: Distance and Ubiquity in Neo-Victorian Popular Culture'. In *Neo-Victorian Villains: Adaptations and Transformations in Popular Culture,* edited by Benjamin Poore, 1–48. Leiden: Brill/Rodopi, 2017.
Poore, Benjamin, and Kelly Jones. 'Introduction to "Swing Your Razor Wide…": Sweeney Todd and Other (Neo-)Victorian Criminalities'. *Journal of Neo-Victorian Studies* 2, no. 1 (Winter 2008/2009): 1–16.
Porter, Roy. *London: A Social History.* London: Penguin, 2000.
Portwine, Timothy [Thomas Peckett Prest]. *The Adventures of Valentine Vaux: Or, The Tricks of a Ventriloquist.* Facsimile of the original, from Gale, Cengage Learning and The British Library. London: E. Lloyd, 44, Holywell Street, Strand; and at 30, Curtain Road, Shoreditch, 1840.
Potter, Franz J. *Gothic Chapbooks, Bluebooks and Shilling Shockers: 1797–1830.* Cardiff: University of Wales Press, 2021.
———. *The History of Gothic Publishing, 1800–1835: Exhuming the Trade.* Basingstoke: Palgrave Macmillan, 2005.
Pykett, Lyn. *The Nineteenth-Century Sensation Novel.* Rev. and Expanded 2nd ed. Tavistock: Northcote House Publishers, 2011.
Quiller-Couch, A. T. 'The Poor Little Penny Dreadful'. In *Adventures in Criticism,* 276–282. New York: Charles Scribner's Sons, 1896.
Raffle, Bryce. 'Burke Street Station'. In *Deadsteam: A Chilling Collection of Dreadpunk Tales of the Dark and Supernatural,* 11–39. Grimmer & Grimmer Books, 2018.
Raine, Sophie. 'Subterranean Spaces in the Penny Dreadful'. In *The Palgrave Handbook of Steam Age Gothic,* edited by Clive Bloom, 61–73. Cham: Springer International Publishing, 2021.
Reports from Select Committees of the House of Commons, and Evidence, Communicated to the Lords, 1842.
Reynolds, George W. M. *The Mysteries of London.* Vol. 1, edited by Dick Collins. Kansas City: Valancourt Books, 2013.
Rose, Jonathan. 'Foreword'. In *The English Common Reader: A Social History of the Mass Reading Public, 1800-1900,* by Richard D. Altick. 2nd ed. Columbus: Ohio State University Press, 1998.

———. 'How Historians Study Reader Response: Or, What Did Jo Think of Bleak House?' In *Literature in the Marketplace: Nineteenth-Century British Publishing and Reading Practices*, edited by John O. Jordan and Robert L. Patten, 195–212. Cambridge: Cambridge University Press, 1995.

———. 'Rereading the English Common Reader: A Preface to a History of Audiences'. *Journal of the History of Ideas* 53, no. 1 (1992): 47–70.

———. *The Intellectual Life of the British Working Classes*. New Haven and London: Yale University Press, 2010.

Ruskin, John. 'The Nature of Gothic'. In *The Stones of Venice*, edited by Jan Morris. Mount Kisco, NY: Moyer Bell, 1989.

Rymer, James Malcolm. *Varney, the Vampire: Or, The Feast of Blood*. Edited by Curt Herr. Crestline: Zittaw Press, 2008.

Shannon, Mary L. *Dickens, Reynolds, and Mayhew on Wellington Street: The Print Culture of a Victorian Street*. Farnham; Burlington: Ashgate, 2015.

Shaw, Vivian. *Strange Practice*. London: Orbit, 2017.

Shea, Victor. 'Penny Dreadfuls.' In *Encyclopedia of the Victorian Era*, edited by James Eli Adams, Tom Pendergast and Sara Pendergast, 185–186. Danbury, CT: Grolier Academic Reference, 2004.

Sherwell, Arthur. *Life in West London: A Study and A Contrast*. London: Methuen & Co., 1897.

Showalter, Elaine. *The Female Malady: Women, Madness and English Culture, 1830–1980*. London: Virago, 1987.

Slater, Michael. *The Composition and Monthly Publication of Nicholas Nickleby*. Menston: Scolar Press, 1973.

Smith, Helen R. *New Light on Sweeney Todd, Thomas Peckett Prest, James Malcolm Rymer and Elizabeth Caroline Grey*. London: Jarndyce, 2002.

Solicari, Sonia. 'Is This Neo-Victorian? Planning an Exhibition on Nineteenth Century Revivalism'. *Neo-Victorian Studies* 6, no. 1 (2013): 180–188.

Sondheim, Stephen, and Hugh Wheeler. *Sweeney Todd: The Demon Barber of Fleet Street. A Musical Thriller*. London: Nick Hern Books, 1991.

Springhall, John. '"Disseminating Impure Literature": The "Penny Dreadful" Publishing Business Since 1860'. *The Economic History Review*, New Series 47, no. 3 (1994): 567–584.

———. '"Pernicious Reading"? "The Penny Dreadful" as Scapegoat for Late-Victorian Juvenile Crime'. *Victorian Periodicals Review* 27, no. 4 (1994): 326–349.

Starkowski, Kristen. '"Our Delectable Works": Characterological Novelty in Penny "Plagiarisms" of Oliver Twist'. *Victorian Review* 45, no. 2 (2019): 271–291. https://doi.org/10.1353/vcr.2019.0059.

Stewart, Garrett. *Reading Voices: Literature and the Phonotext*. Berkeley: University of California Press, 1990.

Straumann, Barbara. 'Der Viktorianische Roman Denkt Seriell: Wiederholung Und Differenz Bei George Eliot'. In *Noch Einmal Anders: Zu Einer Poetik Des Seriellen.*, edited by Elisabeth Bronfen, Christiane Frey, and David Martyn, 162–180. Zurich: Diaphanes, 2016.

Terlaak Poot, Luke. 'On Cliffhangers'. *Narrative* 24, no. 1 (2016): 50–67. https://doi.org/10.1353/nar.2016.0001.

'That Poor Penny Dreadful!' *Punch, or The London Charivari* 109 (7 September 1895): 109.

The London Hermit [Walter Parke]. 'The Physiology of Penny Awfuls'. *Dublin University Magazine* 2 (1875): 364–376.

The Morning Herald. 'The Morning Herald'. 13 September 1831.

'The String of Pearls: A Romance'. In *Sweeney Todd: The Demon Barber of Fleet Street*, edited by Robert L. Mack. Oxford: Oxford University Press, 2007.
Thompson, E. P. 'History from Below'. *Times Literary Supplement* 65 (1966): 275–280.
Thomson, E. S. *Beloved Poison*. London: Constable, 2016.
Tillotson, Kathleen. 'The Lighter Reading of the 1860s'. In *The Woman in White, by Wilkie Collins*, ix–xxvi. Boston: Dover Publications, 1969.
Turner, E. S. *Boys Will Be Boys: The Story of Sweeney Todd, Deadwood Dick, Sexton Blake, Billy Bunter, Dick Barton, et al*. Harmondsworth: Penguin Books, 1976.
Turner, Victor. *The Ritual Process: Structure and Anti-Structure*. New York: Cornell Paperbacks, 1977.
Varney the Vampire or the Feast of Blood. Horror. Demented Features, 2016.
Warner, Michael. 'Publics and Counterpublics (Abbreviated Version)'. *Quarterly Journal of Speech* 88, no. 4 (2002): 413–425.
Wells-Lassagne, Shannon, and Eckart Voigts, eds. *Filming the Past, Screening the Present: Neo-Victorian Adaptations*. Trier: WVT Wissenschaftler Verlag, 2021.
Weltman, Sharon Aronofsky. 'Sondheim's "Sweeney Todd on Stage and Screen"'. *Victorian Literature and Culture* 37, no. 1 (2009): 301–310.
———. *Victorians on Broadway: Literature, Adaptation, and the Modern American Musical*. Charlottesville: University of Virginia Press, 2020.
'What Boys Read'. *Punch, or The London Charivari* 90 (20 February 1886): 96.
Willes, Margaret. *Reading Matters: Five Centuries of Discovering Books*. New Haven; London: Yale University Press, 2010.
Woodmansee, Martha. 'The Genius and the Copyright: Economic and Legal Conditions of the Emergence of the "Author"'. *Eighteenth-Century Studies* 17, no. 4 (1984): 425–448.
Wordsworth, William. 'Book VII: Residence in London'. In *The Prelude*, 169–203. London: Edward Moxon, 1850.
Wynne, Deborah. *The Sensation Novel and the Victorian Family Magazine*. Houndmills: Palgrave, 2001.

INDEX

accent 21, 44
Adventures of Valentine Vaux: Or, the Tricks of a Ventriloquist, The (Portwine) 44
Altick, Richard D. 7, 16
anonymity 23, 46, 53, 54, 57
Arnold, Matthew 8, 20, 25
authorship 23, 46
autobiographies, working-class 14, 18

Bakhtin, Mikhail 44
Beloved Poison (Thomson) 67–70
Bleiler, E. F. 2, 49
Botting, Fred 47, 51, 55, 60
'Burke Street Station' (Raffle) 74–78

canon 7, 70, 77
capitalism 9, 30, 60, 77
cataloguing 7
chapter breaks 38–40
Chartism 3, 6, 21
circulation
    as a concept 10, 11, 61, 81
    as diachronic 10, 65, 78
    as a disruption to the social order 6, 10
    as sales numbers 1, 13
city mysteries 54–56
cliffhanger 39
Cockney 21
Cockton, Henry (*see Life and Adventures of Valentine Vox, the Ventriloquist, The* (Cockton))
Collins, Wilkie 2
communal readings 13–16, 19
consumption practices 5, 9, 16, 18–19, 22–23, 78
contamination metaphor 5, 23, 59
copyright 30, 33, 45
costermongers 14, 15, 19, 21, 78

crime 5, 18, 49, 54
cultural hierarchy 4, 6, 8, 11 (*see also* canon)

Dalziel, Margaret 7
Dickens, Charles 10, 18, 30, 33, 44, 56

education 4, 15, 17–18 (*see also* literacy)
entertainment 2, 29, 30, 34, 40

Foucault, Michel 4, 17
fragmentation 25, 55

Gothic 5, 25, 51, 52, 60, 61, 78 (*see also* London, Gothic image of; urban Gothic)
    legacy and influence 51, 71
    tropes in penny fiction 38, 55, 58

Harmsworth, Alfred 2
Haywood, Ian 7
Hogle, Jerrold E. 51, 61
Hughes, Linda K. (*see* seriality)
humour 30, 45, 58, 72, 73
Humpherys, Anne 7, 54, 55

illustration 15, 34, 36, 45
improvement 6, 18, 68
industrialisation 2, 17, 51, 53, 60

Jacobs, Edward 6, 17, 44
James, Louis 7, 8, 34, 44, 47, 49, 51, 53

Life and Adventures of Valentine Vox, the Ventriloquist, The (Cockton) 42–43
literacy 6, 14, 16 (*see also* education)
Lloyd, Edward 6, 8, 10, 18, 20, 30, 33, 34
London
    contemporary wages in 18
    expansion of 51, 53, 54, 56
    Gothic image of 52–53
    in penny fiction 50, 57, 58

London Labour and the London Poor (Mayhew) 14, 15, 19, 20
Lund, Michael (*see* seriality)

market, literary 2, 3, 10, 18, 22, 30, 48
Marx, Karl 7, 9
mass culture 9, 16, 22, 29
Mayhew, Henry 16, 20, 52, 78 (*see also London Labour and the London Poor* (Mayhew))
Mayhew brothers 69
maze 56–57
metropolis (*see* London)
Mighall, Robert 55, 56
Milbank, Alison 57
moral panics 4, 5
morality (*see also* improvement; moral panics)
  in contemporary view of society 5
  as threatened by penny fiction 5, 6, 66, 69
multimodality 40–46
Mysteries of London, The (Reynolds) 11, 20, 50, 54–57, 74

narration 25, 36–38
neo-Victorianism 65, 70, 72, 78
Newgate Novel 15, 49

Oliphant, Margaret 4
orality 14–16, 41–44 (*see also* communal readings)

Pater, Walter 7
Peckett Prest, Thomas 30, 32, 41
penny bloods, 10 (*see also* penny dreadfuls)
Penny Dreadful (TV series) 65–66, 71
penny dreadfuls
  and contemporary criticism 3–6
  definition 2–3
  in scholarship 6–8
piracy, literary 30, 33, 45

plagiarism 30, 34, 44–45 (*see also* piracy, literary)
Portwine, Timothy 41

radicalism 7, 77 (*see also* Chartism)
reading practices 16 (*see also* communal readings; consumption practices; literacy)
recycling 19, 78
Reynolds, G. W. M. 6, 8, 10, 14, 20, 21, 50, 54, 58, 74
romanticism 23, 49
Rose, Jonathan 13, 16, 18
Ruskin, John 25
Rymer, James Malcolm 46

sensation fiction 29
sensationalism 2, 20, 25, 29, 30, 40 (*see also* multimodality)
seriality 22–25, 40, 66
Springhall, John 2, 3, 5, 7
Strange Practice (Shaw) 70–74
street culture 6, 17, 18
String of Pearls: A Romance, The (Rymer) 11, 35, 38–39, 41, 50, 56–60 (*see also* Todd, Sweeney)

Tidkins, Anthony 74–77
Todd, Sweeney 60, 65, 71 (*see also String of Pearls: A Romance, The* (Rymer))
Turner, E. S. 6

urban Gothic 51, 53–60 (*see also* London)
urbanisation 51–54, 57 (*see also* London)

Varney, Sir Francis 71–74
Varney the Vampyre 11, 51, 70, 71 (*see also* Varney, Sir Francis)

Way of All Flesh, The (Parry) 67
Wicked Cometh, The (Carlin) 80
Willes, Margaret 14, 16, 17

www.ingramcontent.com/pod-product-compliance
Lightning Source LLC
Chambersburg PA
CBHW030142170426
43199CB00008B/175